OLIVES
and
OBLIGATIONS

For Helen
(who suggested the cover)
and Catherine
with love

OLIVES and OBLIGATIONS

Biblical stories, scripts and reflections
Genesis to Nehemiah

Ruth Burgess

wild goose publications

www.ionabooks.com

Contents of book © individual contributors
Compilation © 2018 Ruth Burgess

First published 2018 by
Wild Goose Publications
21 Carlton Court, Glasgow G5 9JP, UK,
the publishing division of the Iona Community.
Scottish Charity No. SC003794. Limited Company Reg. No. SC096243.
www.ionabooks.com

ISBN 978-1-84952-605-0

Cover photograph © Nick Kenrick, Creative Commons licence

The publishers gratefully acknowledge the support of the Drummond Trust,
3 Pitt Terrace, Stirling FK8 2EY in producing this book.

All rights reserved. Apart from the circumstances described below relating to non-commercial use, no part of this publication may be reproduced in any form or by any means, including photocopying or any information storage or retrieval system, without written permission from the publisher.

Non-commercial use: The material in this book may be used non-commercially for worship and group work without written permission from the publisher. If photocopies of sections are made, please make full acknowledgement of the source, and report usage to CLA or other copyright organisation.

Ruth Burgess has asserted her right in accordance with the Copyright, Designs and Patents Act, 1988, to be identified as the author of this compilation and the individual contributors have asserted their rights to be identified as authors of their contributions.

Overseas distribution
Australia: Willow Connection Pty Ltd, Unit 4A, 3–9 Kenneth Road, Manly Vale, NSW 2093
New Zealand: Pleroma, Higginson Street, Otane 4170, Central Hawkes Bay
Canada: Bayard Distribution, 10 Lower Spadina Ave., Suite 400, Toronto, Ontario M5V 2Z

Printed by Bell & Bain, Thornliebank, Glasgow

Contents

Introduction   13

Genesis   15

Exodus   63

Leviticus   91

Numbers   95

Deuteronomy   99

Joshua   111

Judges   117

Ruth   121

1 Samuel   129

2 Samuel   139

1 Kings   153

2 Kings   169

1 Chronicles   179

2 Chronicles   183

Ezra   187

Nehemiah   201

Sources and acknowledgements   206

About the contributors   207

Index of authors   212

Contents in detail

Genesis

Before creation   16
Before the beginning (Genesis 1)   16
Itching to begin (Genesis 1, 2)   18
In the beginning when time began (Genesis 2, 3)   21
Just checking (Genesis 2:15)   23
The tree of what is good and what is bad (Genesis 2, 3)   27
Banishment (Genesis 3:14–24)   29
Dinner (Genesis 4:8)   30
Ark (Genesis 6–9)   31
Noah's prayer (Genesis 7–8)   32
It will be different next time (Genesis 6–9)   34
Noah's hangover (Genesis 9)   35
In years to come (Genesis 6–9)   36
A long journey (Genesis 12:1–9)   37
The stopping and the travelling (Genesis 12)   39
The shame of it (Genesis 12)   41
Keep counting (Genesis 15:1–6)   42
Stargazing (Genesis 15:1–6)   44
Mrs Lot (Genesis 19)   44
Lot's wife (Genesis 19:26)   46
Refuge (Genesis 21:9–21)   47
Abraham, Isaac and the servants (Genesis 22:1–14)   48
Waiting at Moriah (Genesis 22:1–5)   52
Put down the knife, Abraham (Genesis 22:1–14)   52
Rebekah's story (Genesis 24)   54
Until you bless me (Genesis 32:21–30)   55
After Jabbok (Genesis 32, 33)   56
No changing history (Genesis 37)   57
The gossip (Genesis 39)   58

Exodus

The midwives of Egypt (Exodus 1:15–22)   64
Miriam's story (Exodus 2:1–10)   65
Pharaoh's daughter (Exodus 2:1–10)   66
Holy ground (Exodus 3:1–6)   68
Questions and answers (Exodus 2:23–25, 3:10–15, 4:10–17)   69
A reluctant volunteer (Exodus 2:23–25, 3:10–15, 4:10–17)   71
Pharaoh reflects (Exodus 9:12)   73
Are you ready? (Exodus 12:1–4)   74
I am an Israelite. I'm an Egyptian (Exodus 14)   76
Running, running (Exodus 14)   78
The survivor's wife (Exodus 14:23–31)   80
Not counting (Exodus 15:19–21)   81
Enough – simply enough (Exodus 16)   82
Miriam and Mary (Exodus 16)   82
Water from a rock (Exodus 17:1–7)   85
The sort of God they preferred (Exodus 32:1–14)   86
Special places (Exodus 33:7–11)   88
The encounter (Exodus 33:7–11, 34:29)   89
That shine (Exodus 34:29–35)   89

Leviticus

Holy and just (Leviticus 19)   92
You shall not reap to the very edges (Leviticus 19:9–10)   93
Any of your kin (Leviticus 25:35)   94

Numbers

A blessing on and a blessing from (Numbers 6:24–26)   96
He beat me (Numbers 22:21–35)   97

Deuteronomy

The best of your heart (Deuteronomy 4:31)   100
Ten obligations, ten commandments (Deuteronomy 5:1–21)   100
Learning the rules (Deuteronomy 5:1–21)   102
Hope for a better tomorrow (Deuteronomy 24:20)   103
Making the harvest offering (Deuteronomy 26)   104
Choices (Deuteronomy 30:15)   107
On Mount Nebo (Deuteronomy 34:1–12)   108

Joshua

Rahab (Joshua 2:1–21)   112
Gossip about spies (Joshua 2:1–24)   113
No going back (Joshua 3:7–17)   113
Crossing over with wellington boots (Joshua 3)   115
The scarlet cord (Joshua 6:15–25)   116

Judges

Birth of Samson (Judges 13)   118
Boasting in Gaza (Judges 16)   120

Ruth

Returning (Ruth 1)   122
Ruth and Naomi (Ruth 1)   124
The wings of shelter (Ruth 1–4)   127

I Samuel

Don't worry, Hannah (1 Samuel 1, 2:1–21)   130
First encounters (1 Samuel 3:1–21)   131
Who knows best? (1 Samuel 3:1–21)   132
Music therapy (1 Samuel 16:14–23)   134
Winner takes all (1 Samuel 17)   135
And what did Goliath do then, daddy? (1 Samuel 17)   136
Michal's story (1 Samuel 19:20–29 and 2 Samuel 6:16–23)   137

2 Samuel

A joyful noise (2 Samuel 6:1–5)   140
Building buildings (2 Samuel 7:1–17)   142
Rewriting the plans (2 Samuel 7:1–17)   145
Bathsheba's dilemma (2 Samuel 11:1–15)   147
A small lamb (2 Samuel 12:1–9)   149
Rizpah's sisters: mourning as resistance (2 Samuel 21:1–14)   150

1 Kings

What should the king do? (1 Kings 12:1–29)   154
The widow of Zarapeth (1 Kings 17)   155
Ravens above (1 Kings 17)   156
Playing with fire (1 Kings 18:20–39)   158
What are you doing here, Elijah? (1 Kings 19)   159
Translators' paradox (1 Kings 19)   162
The king and the queen and the vegetable patch (1 Kings 21)   162
I am Jezebel (1 Kings 18–21)   165
Growing cucumbers (1 Kings 21)   166

2 Kings

Chariots of fire (2 Kings 2)   170
Naaman and the dirty river of Jordan (2 Kings 5)   172
Advice from a batman (2 Kings 5)   176

1 Chronicles

God's glory (1 Chronicles 16)   180
The substance of what belonged to King David
(1 Chronicles 27:25–31)   181
David's prayer (1 Chronicles 29:10–20)   182

2 Chronicles

Solomon's wisdom (2 Chronicles 9)   184
The Queen of Sheba (2 Chronicles 9)   186

Ezra

I remember it all (Ezra 1–4)   188
The foundation stone (Ezra 1–4)   191
Yes, governor (Ezra 3–6)   193

Nehemiah

Curriculum vitae: Nehemiah, son of Hacaliah (Nehemiah 1–14)   202
This is our story (Nehemiah 9)   203

Introduction

Olives and Obligations began life with a working title of *Genesis to Maccabees*, but as contributions came in it became clear that there was too much material to fit into one book. Consequently this book contains items drawn from Genesis to Nehemiah. The material from Esther to Maccabees will follow in a second book.

The First or Old Testament is a huge collection of books. Despite having read it regularly for over sixty years, in the process of putting this book together I came across characters (six-toed giants) and creatures (chameleons and snails) that I'd previously missed, and some very long names. It was fun.

The material is laid out in biblical order and consists of stories, scripts and reflections based on biblical passages. Some biblical passages attracted more contributions than others, and the collection contains both the familiar and the little known.

Thank you to all the contributors for their rich and imaginative material, which it has been a privilege to edit.

Thank you, too, to the Wild Goose Publications Team – Sandra Kramer, Neil Paynter, Jane Darroch-Riley and Maria O'Neill – for their professionalism and support.

As a child I sang:

*'God has given us a book full of stories …
It was made for his people of old.
It begins with the tale of a garden …'**

Let us begin.

* Maria Matilda Penstone

Tell me a Bible story

What kind would you like?
A love story?
A war story?
An animal story?
A story about a child?

How about Noah and the ark (and the destruction of humanity)?
Or the drowning of the Egyptian army (God's mercy endures forever!)?
Or the Psalmist dashing heads against rocks (the bit we usually leave out)?
Or the bears sent by Elisha (to tear apart impudent boys)?

There are some hideous stories in the Bible.
How do we feel about them?

Do they intrigue us?
Do they offend us?
Do they sadden us?
Do they make us ask questions?

There are some appalling stories in the Bible.
What do we do with them?

Do we tell them in Sunday school?
Do we omit them from the lectionary?
Do we try to explain them?
Do we downright refuse to read them out loud in church?

Is it OK to pick and choose?
What's our criteria for deciding?
Do we need to read the violence along with the peace and justice?
Do we play off the Old Testament against the New?

Stories are important.
Stories are powerful.

Teach us, God, to read the Bible with wisdom and integrity.
Tell us, in the light and in the darkness, the stories we need to hear.

Ruth Burgess

Genesis

Before creation

By God's Word the heavens were made;
by the breath of God's mouth all things came into being.

Psalm 33:6

Before creation, God sits still; draws breath;
asks herself, 'What shall
I sing?'

No polite clearing
of the throat, no
'Excuse me …'

God speaks the storm and the sunset,
the starfish and the octopus,
the sugar-cane and the sycamore,
the butterfly and the locust,
the mole and the tiger,
the woman and the man, and says:
'This is what I mean. Isn't it
glorious fun? Come,
come and play with me
in my creation.'

Brian Morris

Before the beginning (Genesis I)

For seven voices

1: Before the beginning
2: nothing
3: no light
4: no warmth
5: no stars
6: nothing.
7: Nothing but God.

1: At the beginning God
2: God Almighty?
3: God Pre-existent?
4: God Omniscient?
5: God Omnipotent?
6: God Omnipresent?
7: God getting ready to get things done.

1: In the beginning God the Creator
2: God the Maker
3: God the Imaginer
4: God the Dreamer
5: God the Designer
6: God the Artist.
7: You're amazing, God!

1: In the beginning, God made the heavens
2: stars
3: planets
4: suns
5: black holes
6: galaxies.
7: You really went for it, God!

1: In the beginning God made the earth
2: water
3: land
4: vegetation
5: birds and animals
6: fish …
7: I love the butterflies, God!

1: In the beginning God made people
2: a man and a woman
3: made in God's likeness
4: people who could create
5: people who could dream
6: people who could be loving.
7: You made us like you, God.

1: In the beginning and in the making
2: God smiled
3: God hoped
4: God listened
5: God risked
6: God saw.
7: God saw that everything that was made was good.

1: In the beginning God made the heavens and the earth
and then God rested:
2: a day off
3: a breather
4: a walk in the garden
5: a chat with the neighbours
6: a dream for tomorrow.
7: God knew that a story was beginning to be told.

Ruth Burgess

Itching to begin (Genesis 1, 2)

For three voices

A: On the seventh day God rested – phew!

B: But before that
long before that
Day one:
everything formless, everything darkness, everything deep,
and there they were – God in community – itching to begin.

C: And they did –
a wild wind sweeping over the waters
and light
light that was good
light and darkness.
They called the light – day
and the darkness they called – night.

And evening came
then morning
the first day.

A: And so they went on
God in community
swirling and separating the waters
naming the sky.
And evening came again
and morning
the second day.

B: Next they made land
dry land
dry land surrounded by water.
It was good.
They named the land earth
and the waters were called seas.
And plants grew on the earth
plants full of seeds
seeds that could multiply
tiny plants
bushes
huge trees.
And evening came
and morning
the third day.

C: So much to do
but they knew that they needed to get the rhythm right
the dance of the universe
fiery stars and the moon and the sun
day and night
light and darkness
season after season after season
they worked at it
God in community
they sang as they worked
they knew that it was good.

20   Olives and Obligations

A: And evening came
     and morning
     the fourth day.

B: And now it was time to create living creatures
     tiny birds
     and great sea monsters
     creeping things
     crawling things
     flying things
     wild things
     creatures of beauty and wonder.
     God in community
     blessed all of creation
     and made it fruitful.
     It was good.

C: It was good.

A: It was good.

B: And evening came
     and morning
     the fifth day.

C: At the last
     God said:
     Let us make humankind in our image,
     male and female we will create them,
     and let them be stewards of this world
     which we have created.
     And so God made them and blessed them.
     And God gave to every creature that breathes
     the plants of the earth for food.
     God in community looked around
     everything was very good.
     And evening came
     and morning came
     the sixth day.

A: It was done.
Finished.
Living and breathing and dancing.
The heavens and the earth
the plants and the creatures.

B: And God in community blessed the seventh day
and made it holy.

C: And on the seventh day God rested.

A,B,C: Phew!

Ruth Burgess

In the beginning when time began (Genesis 2, 3)

For four voices

1: In the beginning,
2: when time began,
3: God planted a garden in the East.
4: God planted a garden in Eden.

1: In this story, I am a man.
2: I am a woman.
3: I am beyond definition.
4: I am a reptile.

1: At this point in the story I have no name.
2: I have no name either.
3: I have many names.
4: The man named me snake.

1: I live in a garden in Eden.
2: I live with the man.
3: Sometimes, in the evening, I walk in the garden.
4: I live in the garden too.

1: In the garden is the tree of life.
2: In the garden is the tree of knowledge of good and evil.
3: I planted the trees.
4: The trees produce sumptuous fruit.

1: I ate the wrong apple because the woman told me to.
2: I ate the wrong apple because the snake told me to.
3: I saw what happened.
4: I don't eat apples, ever.

1: I blame the woman for tempting me.
2: I blame the snake for tempting me.
3: I know what happened.
4: I blame the trees just for being there.

1: I hid among the trees.
2: I hid with him.
3: I called out to the man, 'Where are you?'
4: I made myself extremely scarce.

1: You know what happened next.
2: If you don't, the story is in Genesis.
3: I gave the man a name: I called him Adam.
   And he gave his wife a name: he called her Eve.
4: Just call me Sydney.

1: It is an old story,
2: a story worth retelling,
3: the story of the Garden of Eden
4: and the story of the snake.

1: It is an old story:
2: a story that raises questions,
3: questions that we still ask,
4: questions that we will always ask in each generation.

1: Who do you blame when you find yourself in a mess?
2: How good are you at forgiving?
3: Who is responsible for the world's troubles?
4: When was the last time you hugged a snake?

Ruth Burgess

Just checking (Genesis 2:15)

Mr and Mrs Adamson are lounging comfortably at home. Mr Adamson is using a tablet computer (which may contain his script). Mrs Adamson is reading a glossy magazine (which may contain her script). Around them lie plates of half-eaten food, and discarded packaging litters the floor. Once Stewart arrives, all three may move around, looking out of imaginary windows.

Mr Adamson: Oh, bother, I'd forgotten all about that.

Mrs Adamson: What's that, dear?

Mr Adamson: Thingummy's coming – from the agency.

Mrs Adamson: The one about extending the patio?

Mr Adamson: No – they came yesterday. They said it's fine to drain the pond, by the way.

Mrs Adamson: Oh good – no more risk of frogs hopping into the salad. So who's coming?

Mr Adamson: Someone from the letting agency.

Mrs Adamson: Oh dear, we haven't got any fruit for him.

Mr Adamson: Fruit? Why would we want that?

Mrs Adamson: It's traditional – you send the landlord some fruit from the garden.

Mr Adamson: But we don't grow fruit any more. You agreed it was too much hassle. Find something else.

Mrs Adamson rummages around in the mess and finds an empty fizzy drink can, which she polishes. During this Stewart appears at the side of the 'stage' and knocks. He carries a briefcase. Mr Adamson goes to greet him.

Stewart: Mr Adamson? Stewart, representing your landlord. I hope you are expecting me.

Mr Adamson: Ah, yes, well – do come in. I'm afraid I can't quite recall the purpose …

Stewart: It's just a routine check, as set out in your tenancy agreement. Good morning, Mrs Adamson.

Mrs Adamson: Good morning. Do take a seat. Would you like some coffee? We've just got a new machine for it. Twelve different options – would you believe it!

Stewart: No, I won't, thank you. *(Sits down and takes a tablet, which may contain his script, and a leather-bound Bible out of his briefcase.)* So how are you finding the property?

Mrs Adamson: Not bad. We've changed it quite a bit, of course, to make it comfortable, and cut down on the maintenance.

Mr Adamson: I expect you saw we've tarmacked the whole of the side now. No more messy dandelions. And once the new patio's been laid, we'll hardly need to step on the grass at all.

Stewart: Talking of steps, I noticed a worrying crack in the doorstep. But let's do things in order. You recall the terms of your tenancy agreement *(touches Bible)*?

Mrs Adamson: Oh, that old thing. We must have a copy somewhere.

Mr Adamson: As I remember, the main point is that the landlord's a generous chap and just wants us to get on and enjoy life.

Stewart: Well, yes, but there is a condition about looking after the property.

Mrs Adamson: And we have. Did you see the kitchen? Everything replaced with the latest models.

Stewart: Ah, is that why there's an old cooker out in the road?

Mr Adamson: Once it's off the property, it's no longer our responsibility.

Mrs Adamson: We've rebuilt the fence, too: makes us much more secure.

Stewart: But you cut down the trees on the northern boundary.

Mr Adamson: That's how we got the wood for the fence.

Mrs Adamson: They make lovely firewood too.

Stewart: Have you planted any replacements?

Mrs Adamson: What – put my hands in that messy dirt?

Mr Adamson: I've done the sums – there's enough to see us through the winter.

Stewart: Have you noticed any impact on the birds?

Mrs Adamson: Now you come to mention it, it is quieter in the mornings.

Mr Adamson: Jolly good too. Noisy, messy creatures.

Stewart: You realise that your tenancy agreement requires you to look after the birds.

Mr Adamson: Surely not! You'll be telling us we should be looking after the bees next.

Stewart: I will. Are there any bees left? I couldn't see any.

Mrs Adamson: I did say to be careful when you did the spraying, dear. I was worried about it getting in the well.

Stewart: Ah yes, the well. Is that in good condition?

Mr Adamson: I presume so. I've never gone down to look. We just run the pump and the water comes up.

Mrs Adamson: We tie the rubbish bags up a bit more carefully now before we drop them down there. We did have a few things getting caught in the pump.

Stewart: What effect does the rubbish have on the water quality?

Mr Adamson: Ah, we're sorting that. We've cleared the ground and we're

	going to build a filter plant, over there, where the apple tree used to be.
Mrs Adamson:	Tell him about the gas, dear. He'll be impressed.
Mr Adamson:	See that pipe there?
Stewart:	In what was originally the vegetable plot?
Mr Adamson:	That's gas. My own discovery. I reckon the source goes right under the house.
Stewart:	Use of explosive substances? Now that *does* require special permission.
Mrs Adamson:	Well, it's there now.
Mr Adamson:	You can't throw us out. We've got lifetime tenancy.
Stewart:	*(rising to leave)* So you have – with a final account at the end. But I suggest you do check your agreement. You can't ask the landlord to repair damage brought about by your carelessness and greed. That crack in the doorstep seems to have grown even since my arrival. *(Prepares to leave.)*
Mrs Adamson:	*(offering the fizzy drink can)* Do take this – as a token of our appreciation.
Stewart:	*(takes can, looking puzzled, and offers business card in exchange)* I'm afraid my report to the landlord will be unfavourable. But do get in touch if you can provide evidence of restoring the property to its original fruitfulness, and I'll be glad to amend it. *(Leaves.)*
Mr Adamson:	Well, really, what an annoying busybody!
Mrs Adamson:	Quite – but this is a bit of a mess, dear. Help me carry these to the well, will you? *(Both exit, taking rubbish with them.)*

Kit Walkham

The tree of what is good and what is bad (Genesis 2, 3)

Once upon a time, a long long time ago, God built a beautiful garden and he called the garden the Garden of Eden. The garden was huge. What do you think God grew in the garden? *(Gather suggestions.)*

Now, God was very fond of fruit and in the middle of the garden God planted lots of fruit trees. There were lemon trees and grapefruit trees and banana trees and pineapple plants and … *(gather suggestions)*.

And all the fruit from God's trees tasted very very good.

There were lots of creatures that lived in God's garden – there were ants and hedgehogs and sparrows and wriggly worms and jackdaws and squirrels and … *(gather suggestions)*.

And there was also a very very crafty snake. The Bible doesn't give him a name but I think we could. What shall we call him? *(Decide upon a name.)*

There were two people who lived in God's garden. The Bible calls one of them, who was a man, Adam, and the other one, who was a woman, Eve. So all the creatures and Eve and Adam and *(name)* the snake lived in God's garden.

God sometimes came into the garden and talked to Eve and Adam.

God showed them two special trees that were planted in the garden. One of these trees was called the tree of life. It was a beautiful tall tree with delicious-looking fruit. 'This is a great tree,' said God. 'You'll love the fruit from this one – eat lots of it.'

The other tree had a longer name. It was called the tree that lets you know what is good and what is bad. 'Leave this tree alone,' said God. 'If you eat from this tree something inside you will die.'

Now *(name)* the snake was always listening to what was going on and he heard God tell Adam and Eve about the two trees.

A tree that lets you know what is good and what is evil, that sounds interesting, thought *(name)*. I'd like to know more about that. But God said if you eat fruit from that tree part of you might die. I don't fancy that.

(Name) was very very crafty. He thought: I could get one of the humans to eat the fruit and I could watch them and see if they die – that would be amusing to watch.

So *(name)* the snake slithered up to the woman who was called Eve.

'Did God say you could eat the fruit in the garden?' said *(name)*.

'God said we can eat nearly all the fruit in the garden,' said Eve. 'We can eat melons and apples and fruit from the tree of life and plums and tangerines and apricots and coconuts and loads more and it's all delicious.'

'Nearly all the fruit,' said *(name)*. 'Why nearly?'

'Well,' said Eve, 'you see that tree over there, the tree next to the tree of life – it's called the tree that lets you know what is good and what is bad and God said that we mustn't touch that one.'

'Why?' said *(name)*.

'Because God said if we eat fruit from that tree, something inside of us will die,' said Eve.

'Well,' said *(name)*, 'that sounds very strange: why would God plant a tree with beautiful fruit on it, and then tell you not to eat it? Perhaps that's God's favourite fruit and God doesn't want to share it … Why don't you try it?' said *(name)*. 'I bet it tastes good.'

Eve wasn't sure what to do.

'Go on,' said *(name)*, 'try it.'

Eve reached up and gently touched the fruit … and then she picked it.

(Name) watched her carefully; she looked fine.

Eve smelt the fruit. It smelt good.

(Name) kept watching.

Eve opened her mouth and she took a bite, and she chewed the fruit and swallowed it.

'Told you,' said *(name)*. 'God must have been teasing: You're not dead, are you?'

Eve looked puzzled. 'I'm not dead,' she said, 'but something inside me doesn't feel right, but I don't know what it is.'

'Interesting,' said *(name),* and he slithered away into the orchard.

Eve felt very strange. I need to go and talk to Adam about this, she thought. I'll get him to try this fruit and see how he feels. And then maybe we need to go and talk to God.

Ruth Burgess

Banishment (Genesis 3:14–24)

Speak it in whispers behind your hand …
the world is no longer what God planned;
that bittersweet fruit has opened our eyes
and changed our vision of Paradise.

It's all over – the secret's out!
The game is up without a doubt.
We broke the rules and we'll have to pay:
Leave this garden, forever, today.

No good accusing each other, because
what does it matter whose fault it was?
For generations we'll take the blame;
our children's children will share our shame.

What can we do? What can we say?
We had it all and we threw it away!
Just one final backward glance –
what wouldn't we give for a second chance?

Mary Gibson

Dinner (Genesis 4:8)

Over here, lads,
dinner!
Fresh too,
and whole,
apart from that big dent in the back of his bonce.
Tuck in.
It's our lucky day.

Why are you hanging back?
Get in quick before the hyenas and jackals arrive.
What do you mean, 'He's one of the lords of creation'?
He was.
Now he's just a veget … Abel.
(Get it? Get it?!)
It looks as if his head's taken a bit of a …
Wait for it! Wait for it!
… Caining.
(Know what I mean?)
Come on,
vultures can't afford to have scruples.

Too late.
Here come some other humans.
We've lost our chance.

Now they're burying him.
All that good meat going into the ground.
Hey, you lot down there!
Waste not, want not!
Fair shares for vultures!

Brian Ford

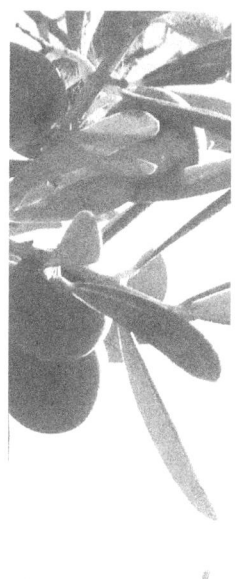

Ark (Genesis 6–9)

Hammer and hone
beat and bang
make and mould
chisel and chip
shape and smooth
forge and fashion
plane and pitch

Gobble and groan
chuckle and chatter
snort and snarl
bleat and bark
caw and cluck
pipe and purr
bellow and bugle
trumpet and trill
cough and croak
warble and whinny
buzz and bray
scream and squawk
hoot and hiss
talk and trust

Rain
relentless,
torrent and tempest and deluge and flood.

Wind
draining and drying, repairing, restoring.

Water receding,

a faint and far-off coo.

Avis Palmer

Noah's prayer (Genesis 7–8)

Lord,
I am really grateful.
Really I am.
We're all safe in the ark
when everyone else is drowned.
And Lord,
I am sorry about the phoenix.
We didn't believe the stories;
we thought they were old wives' tales.
How it got hold of those pieces of flint, I don't know.
Lucky we smelt the smoke in time, eh?
Pity we couldn't save the bird.
Shem reckons it was an evolutionary adaptation
to nesting in the same place in the desert every year.
'The fire would get rid of the parasites,' he says.
Know-all!

And Lord,
I have a rather indelicate matter to raise.
Should I mention this to you?
But you created everything
so you understand about dung.
There are piles and piles of it.
The dung beetles are in heaven –
but I'm literally up to here with it.
The others say that I mustn't pollute the oceans.
And that we'll need it later as organic fertiliser.
But please,
would it be OK to chuck some of it overboard?

And Lord,
they're all moaning about Japheth.
It seemed a logical division of labour at the time,
allowing specialisation, development of expertise.

I look after the mammals, Ham does the birds,
Shem takes the invertebrates
and Japheth the reptiles.
But reptiles only need feeding once a week.
He can witter on as much as he likes about
constantly monitoring environmental conditions,
but the others reckon he's on to a cushy number.
And Shem reckons he's running out of food for the locusts
and they'll turn cannibal if they're starving.
Is he having me on, Lord?

And Lord,
we started off with two rabbits.
Now we've got fifty-four.
I thought I'd give the foxes a treat,
a bit of fresh meat.
'You can't do that!' says Madam.
'Those bunnies are so sweet.'
She didn't object when I fed the baby rats
to the pythons.
Is that the criterion I use to decide
who is to live and who's to die?
Cuteness?

It's enough to drive a man to drink,
it really is.

Brian Ford

It will be different next time (Genesis 6–9)

A monologue by Shem, son of Noah

Angry and sarcastic at first, more thoughtful towards end

It will be different next time. If there is a next time. Dad is of course saying there will be no next time. Apparently that's a promise. Never again. If I'm in charge, it will definitely not be a repeat performance. I won't just stand there without arguing back. I'll have something to say about it! There's going to be a flood, but our little tribe will be fine, so that's no problem then? It's just tough luck for all the rest? I don't think so! Honour your father? How can I honour a man who did not even put up a fight for the sake of our own neighbours, let alone those in the poor drowned cities we will never have a chance to know? What about my poor old friend Aphas? More of a brother than Ham and Japheth have ever been. What about that lamb he loved like a child, and all Aphas' family and their flocks?

So, the waters are subsiding and we have survived. We're all right, so everything's all right? Thank God the disaster happened to someone else? Thank God our lives were worth saving? Nobody else's life really mattered, right?

We cannot yet see what flooding does to the world, but we are beginning to smell it. Does Dad naively think the sea will just go back to where it belongs and leave everything green and shiny and fresh? Does he really see those strange bands of colour in the sky as proof of a happy ever after? They look to me like an upturned ark … God, what a warning! Why should the few stay afloat while the many go under? Who are we to just batten down the hatches while the land is laid to waste? Who has the right to build a cocoon and hide while others have nowhere to run?

God, you've placed your upturned ark in the sky. And you have warned us: it will be different next time.

Jo Love, **Spill the Beans**

Noah's hangover (Genesis 9)

Oh, the light – it is far too bright,
the sun must be high,
it's late.
I've overslept. Not like me.
I just need to get up.

Spinning, it's all spinning,
like I've still got my sea legs
but that can't be possible.
Oh, my head! It is pounding,
like I have not felt since I was young,
a few centuries ago.

What's with this robe over me?
Where did that come from?
Didn't I leave it outside?

The wine! The newly fermented wine!
That's it. Did I make a mistake?
It had quite a kick to it,
but even so, I wasn't expecting this.
Just need to lie still for a few more moments.

What will the children say
when they realise what state I'm in?
Or perhaps they already know …
it is suspiciously quiet out there.

It wouldn't be the first time people talked about me,
the sideways glances as I walked past,
the laughter at the edge of my hearing,
the ridicule heaped high.
I have had enough of that over recent years.

Did I get the last laugh?
Did I feel the temptation to smirk as the waters rose?

I thought I might, but no, only tears fell from my eyes.
It will be some time before laughter caresses the world again.

For now, it is grief and hard work,
relief and rebuilding,
but I am tired, so very tired.

Just a few moments more.

But where did this robe come from?

Peter Johnston

In years to come (Genesis 6–9)

Long ago a little seed fell into fertile soil
and in spring it burst open and made roots in the earth,
and a stem upwards to light.
And over the years it grew, and grew,
strong upwards and strong downwards.
Till a boatbuilder laid his eyes on her beautiful stem,
she was felled, handled with care,
laboured with love, made seaworthy,
and she became a boat,
and they sailed the seas together,
men and boat.
They harvested fish and other creatures from the sea
with which they could feed their families.
Sometimes the sea would take a life
and there would be mourning,
but she sailed again and again.
Till one day she made her final voyage,
and she was laid to rest.
And slowly she is becoming soil again,
fertile soil,
and may grow a tree once more
in years to come.

Roberta van Biezen

A long journey (Genesis 12:1–9)

For 3 voices: narrator (in italics), Abram and Sarah

From long ago, in the Book of Genesis, after the story of Adam and Eve, and Noah and the flood, and the tower of Babel, comes the story of a man and his family whom God called to go on a long journey …

Day 1 – Abram:

God has spoken to me. We are to go on a long journey. God will show me the way to go. I am going to be famous. God is going to bless me. It's so exciting. I must tell Sarah.

Day 1 – Sarah:

Moving – he wants us to move – to leave our friends – to leave our relatives – and to travel to a place that God is going to show him! He's mad! He's seventy-five years old, and I'm not much younger! We're too old to go camping! Does he not realise that his choosing to travel with God will affect all of us?

I blame his father, he was the same, he was always travelling – men! No thought of all the trouble they cause – no thought of who has to do the packing! Now, if God were a woman it would all be very different – far more organised! – I can but dream.

Day 21 – Abram:

We're ready to go. My nephew Lot is coming with us. I think the family insisted he came – they think we're too old to go off on our own – what rubbish – such blatant ageism! Mind you, I hadn't realised quite how many sheep and goats and cattle I have – it took a bit of organising. Sarah's been a bit flustered, but I told her God has it all in hand, we'll be fine.

Day 21 – Sarah:

I'm exhausted. He's been worried about his sheep and goats and cattle – he's had our nephew Lot and all our servants running round in circles. As for the tents, and the clothes, and the food, and the pots and pans, and the water bottles, etc, etc – that of course is all women's work, which I'm expected to organise. He keeps telling me that God will look after us, and I believe him – but, in this household, there are times when God needs a little help from me.

Day 35 – Abram:

We've reached Canaan. There are Canaanites still living here so we've been avoiding the cities. Yesterday we reached Shechem, a very holy place. We came to the sacred tree of Moreh and God came and spoke to me. It's interesting, isn't it, how often God chooses to be near to trees? God told me that one day he is going to give the country of Canaan to my descendants – isn't that amazing?!

I immediately ordered my servants to find stones and build an altar to show that God had appeared to me here. It was very impressive.

Day 35 – Sarah:

I'm still exhausted. All this pitching tents, and finding pots and cooking and catching a few hours sleep and packing up tents and travelling. I told him I'm too old to do camping! He tells me God has spoken to him again. And he's been busy building a huge altar. If he's not careful he's going to have a heart attack!

Day 48 – Abram:

We're up in the hills now, between Ai and Bethel. Quite hard work getting the animals up here. Lot had to do a lot of running around. I felt that God wanted me to build another altar up here, so I did – it's huge – it's a beauty – nobody will be able to miss it!

Day 48 – Sarah:

Nobody told me we were going mountain climbing! What do he and God think they're up to? Though I must admit the view is beautiful. Abram's built another altar. And he's going round telling people we're going to have some prayers. Maybe we're going to stay here for a while. I'd appreciate that. We could sort out the washing and get some much needed rest.

Day 49 and 50 and 60 and 70 and …

They travelled on from place to place to place,
travelling towards the southern part of Canaan …

Ruth Burgess

The stopping and the travelling (Genesis 12)

To follow the Bible reading

Lot: Where next?

Abram: Nowhere, just yet …

Lot: Let me guess. You're stopping again?

Abram: That's right. I'm stopping again.

Lot: Don't you want to see the land?

Abram: That's why I'm stopping. To see the land.

Lot: Not this land. I mean the land God's promised us.

Abram: Well, this could be it. Or some of it.

Lot: You said that at the last place we stopped.

Abram: That's right.

Lot: So why didn't we stay there?

Abram: Stopping and staying isn't everything.

Lot: *(sigh)* You like being on the move then?

Abram: I like being on the move, yes …

Lot: Come on then, let's get on to where we're going!

Abram: There's a time for getting going, and a time for stopping.

Lot:	How long are we stopping for this time, then?
Abram:	I don't know.
Lot:	Let me guess … long enough to build another altar?
Abram:	What a great idea. Yes, we should build another altar.
Lot:	Uncle Abram, why do you build all these altars?
Abram:	It helps me to pray.
Lot:	But you never say anything. You just pick up stones.
Abram:	That's right. The searching and the picking up and the building is my prayer. Words aren't everything.
Lot:	But then you just sit there doing nothing.
Abram:	That's when I do some thinking.
Lot:	Thinking it's another great altar you've just built?
Abram:	Thinking about God, mostly.
Lot:	So what makes you get up and get going again?
Abram:	I don't know. But thinking is not everything. There's a time for travelling again, moving on.
Lot:	So, where next?
Abram:	I don't know …
Lot:	Doesn't God let you know, after all that prayer and thinking?
Abram:	Knowing's not everything.
Lot:	But don't you ever ask questions, Uncle Abram?
Abram:	Oh yes. Just as well answers aren't everything!
Lot:	But God made you a promise. Don't you want to know how it's going to be fulfilled, how you're going to be a blessing?

Abram: Yes, but even promises aren't everything.

Lot: So what's the most important thing then?

Abram: It's all important. The stopping and the travelling, the searching and the building, the praying and the thinking, the words and the altars, the sitting and the silence, the doing nothing and the moving on, the knowing and the not knowing, the questions and the answers, the land and the promise and the being a blessing … it's all important.

Lot: *(after a pause)* Should I give you some peace and quiet now, uncle?

Abram: Only if you want to, my dear nephew.

Jo Love, Spill the Beans

The shame of it (Genesis 12)

My name's Sarah. I was married when I was quite young. No choice about who I married, not in our community. They married me off to Abe, a relative. At first I thought that he was a good man deep down, even if he was a bit of a God-botherer.

Not long after we were married, Abe's father, Terah, decided that the whole family was going to move away to a distant place. I'm not sure why he insisted that we move. Perhaps it had something to do with the civil unrest all around us, the constant fear of war, anyway move we did. The journey was long and tiresome and we had no transport except for a couple of handcarts for our essential belongings. We walked for months and then when it seemed as though we were never going to settle anywhere again, we arrived at a town called Haram, in Syria. We started to settle in, built a house and found pasture for the few animals we had brought with us. Life was just about to get back to normal when Terah died.

It wasn't long before Abe started up bothering God, and the next thing I knew he was telling me that we were going to be on the road again. He told me that God was calling him to be a great leader. 'Are you sure?' I asked. 'You're not a young man any more. Let's just stay here where we are comfortable and we know people. I've made some good friends here.' He didn't listen to me and the next thing I knew we were packing up the handcarts and gathering the animals together once more.

Months of walking most days and sleeping in a smelly sheepskin tent followed. I was exhausted. Just as I thought we were about to settle once again, a famine struck and some of our animals died. Again we were on the move, this time to somewhere more fertile. As we approached a town, Abe took me to one side and said, 'Sarah, you know that you are a very beautiful woman. Any man who sees you will lust after you and want to take you as his wife. They might kill me so that they can have you. Please, Sarah, pretend that you are my sister and save my life.' Being a dutiful wife, I did as my husband asked.

It's hard to speak of what happened next. It still makes me want to cry. It made me feel dirty, humiliated and used, or rather abused. The only man that I had known was Abe, my husband. As we entered the town, the local ruler saw me and set his cap at me. He had a quiet word with Abe and the next thing I knew, he dragged me into his bed. Abe had told him that he could do as he wished with me! I still feel dirty when I think about it. Later I found out that Abe had accepted gifts from the chief in respect of my services. My husband had become my pimp! The shame of it.

Very soon after this the ruler and his family became ill and gave orders that we were to leave town. We were on the move again.

Josie Smith

Keep counting (Genesis 15:1–6)

A story for 3 voices

Voice 1: Do not be afraid, Abram.
I will shield you from danger.
I will give you a great reward.
You will have a child.
You will have many descendants.
Your name will live on.

Voice 2: How many descendants?

Voice 1: Come outside.
Look at the sky.
Try to count the stars.

Voice 2: 1, 2, 3 …
25, 26, 27 …
1045, 1046, 1047 …

Voice 1: Look at the sky and try to count the stars.

Voice 2: 15,377, 15,378, 15,379 …
297,642, 297,643, 297,644 …
479,645, 479,646, 479,647 …

Voice 1: Look at the sky and try to count the stars.

Voice 2: I million and 45, 1 million and 46, 1 million and 47 …
234 billion 14 million and sixty-two, 234 billion 14 million and sixty-three, 234 billion 14 million and sixty-four …

Voice 1: Look at the sky and try to count the stars.

Voice 2: Thirty-three trillion, forty-four quadrillion, one hundred octillion.

Narrator: Abram trusted God.
God loved him and God blessed him.
The love of God is infinitely strong and tender and full of blessing.

Voice 1: Look at the sky. Try to count the stars.

Voice 2: 1, 2, 3, 4 …

Narrator: Do not be afraid.
God loves us.
Keep counting.

Ruth Burgess

Stargazing (Genesis 15:1–6)

Ailsa had been learning about the stars in the sky. She knew now where to look for the star pattern called Orion and the one called the Plough. She knew, too, that people in other countries could see different patterns of stars at different times of the year, and sometimes they called the patterns different names.

Adults, as well as children, seemed to be fascinated by the stars. Scientists talked about them on television. People often made new discoveries about stars and planets. Some countries sent rockets into space.

In the city, it was sometimes hard to see the stars because there were too many streetlights around, but Ailsa knew one easy thing that helped. If you closed one eye and looked through the inside of a toilet roll with the other eye, you could see the night sky a lot more clearly.

Ailsa thought that she would like a telescope when she was older. She would be able to sit in the garden at night and look at the stars and she'd enjoy that.

Ailsa's Sunday school teacher had told her class about a verse in the Bible where God had told Abram to look up to the sky and to try to count the stars. Ailsa wondered what Abram had thought when God asked him to do that.

One day, Ailsa might have a telescope of her own.

Ruth Burgess

Mrs Lot (Genesis 19)

Narrator: Let us listen to the wife of Lot, who is usually remembered for disobeying God by looking back on her town.

> *I am Mrs Lot, Lot's wife. I am standing here looking back to my friends in Sodom. This is the second time I've had to leave my home and my friends. Years ago I had to leave Haran without any explanation. I was very young, but around me were a good group of young*

women like me. We met at the well to fill our buckets. When I was waiting my turn, there was time to talk to the other women, to laugh, to gossip and simply enjoy the company and solidarity. Each day began with sharing and friendship.

Then, one day, Lot told me we were leaving Haran with his uncle Abram and Sarai, his wife. God had told them to leave Haran and go to Canaan.

On the long trek Sarai and I were often together, and helped one another. And Sarai confided to me that she, too, had not really wanted to leave.

We lived in tents, travelling with our cattle, letting the animals graze. Then, when our herdsmen got angry with each other, Abram and Lot separated. We had to go, and moved to Sodom, where we found good land.

Very soon I met new friends at the well. I felt accepted and at home again. We were such a good group of women – so I don't understand why God is punishing the town. Lot pushed me out of the house this morning, saying: 'Hurry up! Take your stuff – we must leave!'

So now here I stand, looking back, staring into the flames of Sodom and crying.

God, why are you doing this? My family has left me behind to find a safe place. God, have mercy – stop the fire!

Narrator: And suddenly Mrs Lot's feet were stuck in the ground and she could not move.

Never mind! I am so tired, sad and hopeless that I want to die, or at least sleep till my life ends. God, have mercy.

Narrator: And Mrs Lot closed her eyes and fell to the ground. Later, there was a strange pillar of salt left there. People said: 'This is Mrs Lot. She did not obey God, so she became a pillar of salt.'

Elisabeth Christa Miescher

Lot's wife (Genesis 19:26)

Which of us could have walked away
from the stone house, the well,
the busy market of gossip
at the command of some god
who talked only to our husband?

He never spoke our names
or the names of our daughters,
from not knowing or not caring.
We threshold-sweepers,
lamb-cookers, water-carriers
never pausing to rest.

The city was a cesspool
but one with a thousand lamps lit at dusk.
There was beauty in the pomegranates
stacked next to the smooth mud walls
we gathered to repack every year.

Which of us would not have turned
to remember those neighbours
and dismiss familiar squabbles?

Which of us would not have stopped
so briefly, just this once, to say:
There, that was my life.
To pause and say, Here,
now I am ready for the new.

Cara Bertron

Refuge (Genesis 21:9–21)

A reflection inspired by Hagar's story, for a service on domestic violence

It was terrifying to leave.

All the time I was afraid he'd come after me. He'd always said he'd kill me if I left, and after the beatings he'd given me I could believe it. But I couldn't stand any more, and when he started on the children I knew I had to go, to protect them.

I didn't really know where to go or what I could do. But a friend had told me about a refuge, and given me a phone number – said it was a safe place for someone like me, and they'd help me. I didn't even know where it was.

I was shaking so much when I rang the number I could hardly speak; but they told me where to go, and said someone would meet me.

When I got there it was shabby and tucked away; and inside, it was scruffy and noisy, with all the kinds running around. There were no men, and they told me it had to be secret, so they couldn't come after us. I never realised there were so many other women in the same boat.

Gradually I got to know some of them; we shared our stories as our children began to play together. Slowly I started to feel safe, and to feel I counted again. People listened to me, took me seriously.

Sometimes I think about going back. I try to kid myself it would be different now; I'd be stronger and stand up to him, and we'd be a family again. Then I remember him hitting the kids, and I see how the cringing look of fear is beginning to fade from their eyes – and I think, *No, I've seen things differently now – I can't go back.*

It's still really scary. I'd like to find my own place, start again – and maybe one day – soon – I'll feel strong enough.

Jan Berry

Abraham, Isaac and the servants (Genesis 22:1–14)

The servants

We do as we're told.
We always do as we're told,
we're servants and servants do as they're told.

It was early in the morning, very early,
when Abraham our master called us
and told us we were going on a journey.

There was us
and Abraham
and Abraham's son Isaac
and a donkey.
Abraham's wife Sarah stayed at home.

We took wood with us,
wood for an offering.
Abraham our master is very religious.

It was a long journey.
It took three days.
We had to camp each night,
us, Abraham, Isaac and the donkey.

On the third day
Abraham said to us:
'Stay here with the donkey.
Isaac and I will go and worship
and we will come back to you.'

Abraham took the wood from the donkey's back
and gave it to Isaac to carry,
and Abraham took fire
from the fire we'd made to keep ourselves warm
and he took a knife.
And he and Isaac walked on together up a mountain.

We stayed by the fire.
We knew that Abraham was going to make an offering,
but he had no lamb to offer;
it was all rather odd.

We waited a long time by the fire.
We'd hobbled the donkey and kept the fire going.
We waited and waited.
Abraham had told us to wait,
so we kept on waiting.

It was getting dark
when we saw them returning in the distance.
They both looked very tired –
you could tell something had happened to them –
and there was blood on Abraham's clothes but none on Isaac's.

They said very little that night.
They seemed wary of each other.
The next morning we packed our things together
and set off home for Beersheba.

On the journey home
Abraham and Isaac walked with each other.
They talked a little, but were mostly silent.

Something had obviously happened to both of them,
something important,
something too important to be discussed with servants,
something that had changed them.

In the days that followed rumours abounded.
Sarah seemed really upset
and kept Isaac very close to her.

People asked us what had happened but we could tell them very little.
It was between Isaac and Abraham what had happened on the mountain.
Between Abraham and Isaac and that God they believe in.

Isaac

When I think of that day I shudder.
It was years ago
but I remember it as clearly as yesterday:
that trip up the mountain,
me asking questions,
dad strangely silent.

How would you feel
if your dad,
for no reason,
tied you up,
and picked up a knife
and raised his hand in the air
and you thought he was going to kill you?

Yes, we talked about it afterwards;
we talked about it a little on the way home.
At times dad seemed as scared as me about what had happened
but he still trusted that God he believed in.

Mum was incandescent
when I told her what had happened –
she was so angry she didn't talk to him for days.

I was wary of him after that,
our relationship changed, it had to really.

I sometimes hear people talking about the God of Abraham and Isaac
as if me and dad had the same kind of trust in God – I don't think we do.

When I think of that day I still shudder.
It was years ago
but I remember it as clearly as yesterday,
that trip up the mountain.

Abraham

When I heard God calling me
I always answered:
'Yes, here I am.'

That day part of me wished I hadn't.

I will go down in the history of my people
as the one who was obedient to God,
as the one who God blessed.

I will also go down
as the one who was ready to sacrifice his son
when God asked him to.

Isaac, Isaac,
what did I do to you that day?

God, what was I thinking of?

God, what were you thinking of?

God, please never ask me to do anything like that ever again.

Ruth Burgess

Waiting at Moriah (Genesis 22:1–5)

If you ask me, the old boy has finally flipped.
He always was a bit strange.
Suddenly deciding to leave Ur,
go out into the wilderness
and take all of us with him.
Do you remember that odd business
when he cut up those animals
and sat with the pieces all night?
And when he thought those three visitors at Mamre
were God?
Now here we are, left in the middle of nowhere.
He and Isaac have gone off with the wood and the fire
to carry out a burnt offering.
I reckon he's a couple of sheep short of a sacrifice.
Mind you, he's got that great knife with him
so something's going to die.
… Or someone.
… You don't think?
Perhaps we should say a prayer for Isaac?
Can't do any harm, can it?
We've got nothing else to do.

Brian Ford

Put down the knife, Abraham (Genesis 22:1–14)

This is a very old, important, yet difficult story.

A central story about Abraham, revered as the Father of faith for Jews, Christians and Muslims.

He climbs the mountain with his loved and longed-for little boy Isaac, whose name means laughter. There with firewood and a knife in his hand, he binds him, with every intent to kill, because he believed that God had told him to.

I wonder if Sarah knew what he was up to. I think not. She would have gone ballistic! 'Oh look,' they tell you, 'what a hero! What a great example of obedience to God!'

No, I don't buy it!

But perhaps what makes Abraham the hero here isn't that he was willing to kill Isaac, but that he didn't.

He had thought this was what God wanted. Many other people at the time practised human sacrifice. At a time when wives and children were considered possessions, it meant giving everything to God. But he was wrong.

Just in time, he listened to another voice, the voice of an angel, 'Put down the knife, Abraham. Do not harm one hair on his head. This is not what God wants.'

Abraham had the courage to realise that he had been wrong, untie his trembling little boy and climb down that mountain.

Yet too many times since then, Abraham's children have wielded their knives in response to what they thought was God's command: the Crusades, 9/11, Northern Ireland, Israel/Palestine. Amid the clamour, angels' voices so often go unheeded.

Stand up for the Isaacs of the world. Challenge harm done in the name of faith. Let us dare to be the voice of the angel: 'Put down the knife, Abraham, this is not what God wants.'

Liz Delafield

Rebekah's story (Genesis 24)

I was fifteen. I knew that my father was looking about for a husband for me, and I was both excited and scared by the prospect. Part of me was terrified at the thought of leaving home and going to a complete stranger. Part of me longed for romance and adventure, which I didn't believe would come from a marriage to any of the suitable men in the neighbourhood. Men I had known all my life, my brother's boring friends. So I was dreaming and worried all at the same time.

It began like any other day. When I went to the well for water as usual, I had no idea how different everything was going to be. As I approached the well, I saw the camel train. The leading man looked as if he had been praying. He stood up when he saw me. I thought perhaps he was the chief servant of some great man. He was certainly too important to do the women's work of drawing water, and as I brought the full water jar from the well he said, 'Please, will you give me some water?' 'Of course,' I said, swinging the water jar from my shoulder, for hospitality was the custom of our house. 'I'll get some for your camels and servants as well.' He looked delighted, more than the service seemed to warrant, but watched me in silence. When I had finished, he took out some really expensive jewellery, a nose ring and bracelets, and put them on me. 'Tell me,' he said, 'who is your father? Will I be able to stay in his house tonight?' 'I am the daughter of Bethuel, the son of Nahor and Milcah,' I said. 'There is plenty of room for guests in my father's house, and fodder and stabling for your camels too.' He knelt to pray again. 'Thank you, God, for doing what I asked.'

Astonished and excited, I rushed home, as fast as I could with a full jar of water. I ran to my mother. 'Look at these bracelets and this nose ring! There's a man at the well who gave me them after I had given him a drink and water for his camels. He asked me who my father was, and when I told him, he seemed really pleased.' My brother Laban overheard me, and dashed off to find the man and bring him home for the night.

Later that evening, my parents and brother came to me. My father said, 'The man is the steward of my uncle Abraham. He has been sent by his master to find a wife for his son Isaac from among his family. God's sign has shown him that you are the right wife for Isaac. Do you agree to go with him?' I thought for a moment. 'Yes,' I said, 'if it is God's will.' Abraham's servant had more gifts for me, jewels and fine textiles. There were gifts for my parents and brother as well.

That night I couldn't sleep for excitement. Here was a romance indeed! But I was a little afraid too. It was such a long way to go, and I knew nothing of this man Isaac, though he was my cousin.

In the morning the man wished to be gone immediately, but my parents wanted him to stay for a few days. They asked me what I wanted to do. I drew a deep breath. Would a week make parting any better – or any worse? 'I am willing to go now,' I said. So my belongings were quickly packed. My old nurse and some of the young servant girls came with me, and we set out.

It was a long journey. At last, as we entered the land of Canaan, I saw a man approaching us. The camel train stopped and I got down. 'Who is that man?' I asked the steward. 'That is my master, Isaac,' he said. At once, I veiled myself, as I listened to the steward telling Isaac the story of his quest. Isaac approached me. 'Come,' he said. 'Let us go to the tent that was my mother's. We will hold the marriage feast and we shall be happy.'

Fiona Middlemist

Until you bless me (Genesis 32:21–30)

When Jacob faced the dusk in dread,
not knowing what the day would bring,
he sent his company ahead,
and waited by the Jabbok spring.

A man stepped out of nothingness.
They wrestled till the stars grew dim.
And seeing Jacob's stubbornness,
he touched his thigh, and crippled him.

The man said, 'Jacob, let me go:
the dawn is rising into day.'
But Jacob gripped, and told him: 'No:
until you bless me, here we stay.'

'From this day on, by gift and right,
let people call you Israel:
in memory that one long night
you wrestled God, and fought him well.'

'Since you have my true name,' he said,
let me know yours to seal the gift.'
The stranger smiled, and shook his head,
and silent as the dawn he left.

Roddy Cowie

After Jabbok (Genesis 32, 33)

Any other man would have told the truth,
or at least made up a plausible story.
We know what really happened.
He'd heard his brother was on his way with a squad of heavies.
(I don't need to remind you how often
he'd conned the poor blighter when they were lads.)
He was scared witless,
had a few drinks,
imagined he was fighting some sort of supernatural power,
fell in the brook
and wrecked his hip.
But not our Jacob.
Would you believe he was fighting with an angel?
(I wouldn't.)
Would you believe he wrestled with God all night
and finally wrung a blessing out of Him?
I think we have desert-sized delusions of grandeur here,
with an ego the size of the Great Pyramid.

And all that elaborate messing about
sending gifts of livestock,
splitting us up into small groups
(with his precious Rachel and her stuck-up brat

safely at the rear).
No wonder they call him Twister!

Then along comes dear, stupid old Esau.
Nice as pie.
No trouble at all.

And Jacob reckons God has chosen him to be the Father of a great nation.

I hope they don't inherit his behavioural characteristics.

Brian Ford

No changing history (Genesis 37)

He was a dreamer,
our Joseph.
Dreams are strange things sometimes,
and if he'd been older and wiser
he might have kept his dreams to himself.

Nobody wants a spoilt baby brother –
and a spoilt teenager is even worse.
Mind you,
dad giving him that long robe
hadn't helped much, had it?
Though at least he'd seen through
the sun, moon and stars routine
and had told Joseph to mind his mouth.

We got our chance in Dothan
when Joseph came out alone to find us.
Most of us would have happily killed him
but Reuben wouldn't have it,
and his word goes.

We stuck Joseph down a well instead.
It was a dry one,

and it wasn't very deep,
but deep enough for him not to climb out on his own.

As chance would have it
some traders came along the path
and Judah suggested selling Joseph to them as a slave.

We did OK.
Twenty pieces of silver.
And it was Goodbye, dreamer.
Have an interesting life!

We showed dad Joseph's robe.
We'd smeared it with animal blood
and dad drew his own conclusions.

Dad's never really got over it,
but there's no way we can tell him
what really happened.
I'm ashamed of what we did,
but there's no changing history,
is there?

Ruth Burgess

The gossip (Genesis 39)

Morning, Kiya.

Morning, Tye.

Have you heard about Joseph?

Heard what about Joseph?

Potiphar's put him in prison.

Joseph – in prison – why?

Well ……

Well what?

Well, according to Merities –

Merities – she's always telling stories – you don't want to listen to her.

According to Merities – Mrs Potiphar has been up to her old tricks.

Tell me more.

I thought you didn't want to hear any of Merities' stories?

Shush now – this is interesting – get on with it.

Well …… You know how Potiphar had put Joseph the Israelite in charge of our household?

Yes.

And you know that Joseph changed all kinds of things and made life fairer and better for everybody.

Yes – he's a great organiser – life's been good since he's been in charge.

Well – Mrs Potiphar didn't like it.

Why ever not?

Well, think back, Tye. Before Joseph came she was in charge of the household: she organised the servants, made the decisions, did what she liked and …

And …

And Merities says that the other captains' wives have been teasing her, telling her she's not in charge any more.

How on earth does Merities know that?

You know Merities – she has her ways. Anyway, Merities says that Mrs Potiphar decided that Joseph had to go.

So what did she do?

Well, you know that Joseph is handsome and good-looking.

Mmmmmmm ...

Well, every time Mrs Potiphar saw Joseph, she invited him into her bedroom.

Into her bedroom? Whatever for?

Tye! Use your imagination!

Ooooooh!

Oooooh indeed! – but Joseph wasn't having any of it – he told her that Potiphar was his master and he wasn't going to let his master down.

She wouldn't like that.

She didn't!

So what happened?

Well, Mrs Potiphar kept inviting him into the bedroom and he kept saying no – and the more he said no the angrier she became and then yesterday ...

Yesterday?

Yesterday, when there were no other slaves or servants around, she grabbed him!

She didn't! What did Joseph do?

He ran.

Don't blame him, what else could he do?

He ran, but she'd grabbed his coat and ...

And?

And she went and found some of her favourite servants and told them that Joseph had tried to force her into the bedroom and that she'd screamed and that he'd run away and left his coat.

The lying b ......

Tye! Language!

Sorry, Kiya – but she's a wicked woman – what happened next?

Well, she waited for Potiphar to come home – and she showed him Joseph's coat – and she told him her version of what had happened.

Did Potiphar believe her?

He did – and he was so angry that he put Joseph in the king's prison – and not many people come out of there in one piece!

Poor Joseph.

Yes and poor us – without Joseph we're back to life organised by Mrs Potiphar, and that's not good for any of us.

No – it's not.

Oh, and Merities heard one more thing.

What was that?

She said that the prison jailor has taken a liking to Joseph.

That's good.

And he's talking about putting Joseph in charge of the prison.

Good for Joseph, but let's hope Mrs Potiphar never finds out.

Why should she, Kye? After all, nobody tells stories around here.

Ruth Burgess

Exodus

The midwives of Egypt (Exodus 1:15–22)

Shiphrah is standing in the middle of the worship space. Puah enters looking agitated, carrying a scroll.

Shiphrah: What's up, Puah?

Puah: Have you seen this?

Shiphrah: What is it?

Puah: A new directive from Pharaoh to all Egyptian midwives.

Shiphrah: That's us then. What does it say?

Puah: 'Kill all the Hebrew baby boys, as soon as they are born.'

Shiphrah: What! Who does this man think he is?

Puah: He's the Pharaoh, the ruler of our land.

Shiphrah: He's still a man though. What does he think he knows about midwifery? Killing babies? We can't do that!

Puah: Wasn't the mighty Pharaoh put on earth to guide us in the ways of the gods?

Shiphrah: But how would any god want anyone to kill a baby?

Puah: I understand what you're saying. It just doesn't seem right, does it?

Shiphrah: Agreed then. So we just carry on as usual. No killing, just being there when women need us like we've always done.

Puah: But won't he be suspicious? We'll be in for it when he finds out.

Shiphrah: Look, men, even Pharaohs, don't really know what goes on. We'll have to think of something.

Puah: Yes. Look, I read an article in the *Daily Pyramid*. It said that the Hebrews aren't like Egyptians. It's like they're a different species. That's why it's OK to make them drag those heavy stones across

	miles of desert. They don't feel pain like the rest of us.
Shiphrah:	How ridiculous! Isn't it about time you stopped reading that rag?
Puah:	No, you misunderstand me. When Pharaoh asks why we didn't kill any Hebrew babies, we claim that the Hebrew women are different.
Shiphrah:	Yes, they don't feel pain like us and they give birth all by themselves, and so don't need to call for a midwife.
Puah:	Right, let's go then, business as usual.
Shiphrah:	No nonsense, no killing, just helping women like we always do.

Liz Delafield

Miriam's story (Exodus 2:1–10)

I had two younger brothers. Aaron was nearer my age and we were good friends; as I got older, I realised that we were slaves – only able to do what the Egyptians told us to do, or not to do. Dad worked hard making bricks but we had enough to eat and Aaron and I would play happily with the other children and attend lessons, learning to read and write and about our Jewish faith and history.

But by the time mum was pregnant with the next child, the work had got much harder – and the Egyptians had ordered that all Jewish male babies should be killed at birth. We prayed hard that the baby would be a girl, but it was a boy; we managed to hide him for three months, but then something had to be done or the Egyptians would have found him and killed him. Then mum and I hatched a plan – we made a basket out of papyrus and coated it with pitch, put the baby in the basket and floated it in the reeds in the river near to where the princess came to bathe. We hoped she would find him and save him, but even if not, we had nothing to lose!

I stood and watched. She *did* find him and she wanted to keep him, even though she realised that he was a Jew, son of a slave. Mum and I had thought that she probably wouldn't have anyone to feed him, so very nervously I went forward and asked the princess if she needed a wet nurse – of course she did, but didn't know where to find one – well I did! So mum went to the palace to care for her own son until he was old enough for the princess to look after him! It gave mum a chance to talk to him about his family and our faith and history, just as she had to us.

It was the princess who gave him his name – Moses – it means 'drawn out', because she drew him out of the water.

Thinking about it, when we were praying for a girl, perhaps we should just have prayed that God would care for the baby – because God did, giving us the ideas and the princess a loving heart. We didn't know it then, but God had a special plan for this baby, my little brother.

Helen Barrett

Pharaoh's daughter (Exodus 2:1–10)

I had a privileged life, I know that.
I could have anything I wanted.
I had female attendants to look after me,
to attend to all my needs.
But I was lonely.
I couldn't share in their gossip.

Sometimes I would go down to the river to bathe.
I didn't go alone, of course,
my attendants came with me.
They weren't permitted to bathe.
They just had to stand or walk along the river and watch,
have the towels ready for when I came out
and help me to dry and dress.

One day as I went down to the river I heard a baby cry.
Then I noticed the basket in the reeds and realised a baby must be there.
I sent my slave girl to fetch it.
It was a beautiful baby, a boy.
I felt sorry for him.
I wanted to keep him.
To have a child to love.

But then I realised why the child was there.
It must belong to one of the Hebrew women.
My father had ordered that all the boys born to Hebrew women
were to be killed.
The Hebrew slaves were getting too numerous
and he was afraid they would rebel
or even worse, join his enemies if war broke out.

While I was thinking whether it was sensible to keep him,
a young girl appeared from nowhere.
She must have been hiding in the reeds.
Was she guarding the baby?
Had she been watching us?
She approached me.
She was either very brave or very foolish.
I could have had her killed for daring to speak to me.

She asked me if she should go and find a wet nurse for the child.
I realised then how impracticable it would be for me to keep the child.
I had no milk to give it.
This was an answer to my dilemma.
She would find a woman who would care for the baby
until he was weaned.
Then he could come to me and be brought up as my son.

The girl soon returned with a woman.
I guessed she was the mother of both the baby and the girl.
I felt sorry for them.
The prospect of your baby being killed must be awful.
I would save this one.
I gave the baby to its mother
and I also gave her some money to nurse him for me.

Perhaps there was a purpose in this child living
when so many of the other Hebrew boys had been killed.

When the child was weaned the woman brought him to me.
He grew up in the royal household, my adopted son.

I wonder if one day he will want to return to his own people.

Margaret Roe

Holy ground (Exodus 3:1–6)

Mostly the spiritual life is about paying attention. Paying attention to our breath moving in and out of our fragile bodies and to the heart that beats within. Paying attention to the sunrise and sunset of each blessed day and to the rhythm of the seasons ... winter, spring, autumn, summer. Paying attention to the rhythms of our lives ... birth, life, death, resurrection. In that intention to being fully present, we become awake to the Holy's movement in it all.

Moses, the shepherd, tending his sheep in the wilderness, was living the distracted life we all live. Keeping an eye on a flock of wanderers and stubborn creatures, his days must have been filled with responsibility, boredom, menial tasks and a desire to be anywhere other than the present moment. His mind must have been numbed by the drudgery of it.

And then the bush started burning. He watched as it kept sending flames into his everyday, ordinary life. And it just wouldn't stop. He was forced to pay attention. His eyes were opened to God's presence – there in the midst of moments which before seemed dull, uninteresting, ordinary. His ears were opened to the voice that speaks through our often mundane existence, calling our names, awakening us to the Presence that is always there ... even when we are too dulled to notice. Breath. Fire. Presence. Awakening. Naming. The 'I Am' shows up.

The only response that seems sensible, humble, wise is to take off our shoes, our sandals, our hiking boots, our stilettos and allow our bare feet to touch with reverence the dear, beautiful earth that is home to our living. Grounded in the One who is always present (even when we refuse to notice) we hear the voice that echoes through the universe: 'Holy ground ... holy ground ... holy ground.'

Sally Howell Johnson

Questions and answers
(Exodus 2:23–25, 3:10–15, 4:10–17)

Moses questions

O God, why do you have to pick on me?
There are much better people who could do this work of yours!
C'mon, Lord, there are people who are used to speaking in public.
People who are fearless, passionate, persuasive.
Who stick their neck out for the sake of others
and seem to be filled with your Spirit,
making them erudite, eloquent, articulate.
As for me, I am shy, and I get flummoxed when I stand up in public.
You know I have a stutter
and every word takes an age to be formed in my mouth.
You know that I get all muddled in my thinking.
You know that I am, well, not the brightest in the classroom,
and that I could never stand up to Pharaoh and his thugs.

C'mon, God, there are hundreds who are more qualified than me:
people who understand politics and sound bites,
people who understand our laws and religion better than I do,
people who are good at strategy and planning,
people who are good at getting others onside,
people who are just soooo much better than me!
Please, God, pick a winner and not a loser like me.

This is important to get right, God,
for this person will speak for the nation and needs to be a leader.
I can't do it.
My brother would be better than me.
In fact, anyone would be better than me!
O Lord, I know it is an honour and all that,
but please choose someone else – anyone else – just not me.

God responds

Moses! Moses! Moses!
All I hear are excuses – and more excuses!
Don't you think I considered all the possibilities?
Don't you think I knew who all the potential candidates were?
You have insider knowledge of Pharaoh and his people.
You were brought up as one of them,
you have more knowledge and understanding than anyone.
Your stepmother was an Egyptian princess,
and the Egyptian officials know your name,
and Pharaoh will listen to what you have to say … eventually!

Moses, trust me on this:
I am making myself known to you.
I know what you are like:
I know every hair on your head.
I know your weaknesses and your strengths,
your gifts and talents, your limitations.
I know the times you have let me down,
and I know the times you have remained faithful.
I chose you because I know you are the right man for this job.
I will be with you every step of the way.
I will give you a staff as a symbol of my presence.
So, when you speak, I will put the words in your mouth.
When I call on you to act, I will be the one taking the lead.
When I make demands on Pharaoh, you will be listened to.
When I promise to be with you, I will be there every moment of the way.
You are the one for this job.
You have met me face to face, and you know I am faithful to my word.
So I am not going to pick your brother Aaron.
I am not going to pick anyone else to do the job.
I am choosing you, because you are exactly right for this job!
Accept it, cherish it and live it.
I AM has spoken!

John Murning, Spill the Beans

A reluctant volunteer
(Exodus 2:23–25, 3:10–15, 4:10–17)

When the teacher asked for a volunteer
to cut shapes out for a maths lesson,
Martin was always first to put his hand up and volunteer.
He liked cutting things out.

When the coach at Lisa's gymnastic club asked for a volunteer
to demonstrate a forward roll,
she would jump up and down excitedly,
because she was the best in the club
at doing forward rolls and cartwheels.

When Billy's team got a penalty in a football match,
he always volunteered to take it,
because he had never missed a penalty kick.

When the head teacher asked for someone
to recite a Robert Burns poem
in the Schools District Burns Competition,
Heather volunteered every time,
because she loved poetry
and knew many of Robert Burns' poems off by heart.

What things would you volunteer to do? …

Would you volunteer to be a buddy at school?

Would you volunteer to swim in the swimming competition?

Would you volunteer for something only if you got a reward at the end of it?

Or are you the one who hides behind someone else whenever a volunteer is asked for?

Moses didn't volunteer to do anything.

God picked him out because he thought he would be the best person to do this job.

It was not going to be an easy job.

The people of Israel had been slaves in Egypt for a long time and God needed someone to ask Pharaoh, the leader of all Egypt, to let the Israelites go.

However, Moses was a reluctant volunteer.

He pleaded with God,
he begged God,
he tried to persuade God
that he was not the man for this job.
He told God he was too shy.
He told God he did not have a strong voice.
He told God that no one would listen to him.
He told God that his brother Aaron would do a better job.
He told God that *anyone* would do a better job than he would.

Yet God knew Moses better than anyone.

He knew that Moses knew the Egyptian language because he had grown up in the Egyptian palace.

He knew that Moses knew the Pharaoh and many of the other important people in Egypt.

He knew that Moses had a real heart for the Israelites, as he was born to an Israelite mother and father, and had heard all the stories about the suffering they had endured for a long, long number of years.

God promises Moses that he would be with him.

He would help him to find the right words. He would help him do the right things.

He would give him the courage and the strength he needed.

So reluctantly, Moses agreed to do the job God asked him to do,
and, believe it or not,
at the end of all the talking and all the discussions
and all the toing and froing,

Pharaoh let the Israelites go,
and Moses took them on a journey toward the promised land.

However, that is a story for another day.

John Murning, Spill the Beans

Pharaoh reflects (Exodus 9:12)

Hey, Moses, can you hear me? They're turning out the lights in the upper galleries of the museum.

It's always dark and quiet after the parties of schoolchildren leave. When they tap their fingers on the walls of my glass coffin, it reminds me of the rain in the Nile Delta.

I so wish I could feel moisture on my face again. My own tear ducts have been dry for over three thousand years now, and I fear that I would drown inside my bindings if I were to weep all the tears that I owe. As if for added punishment, during the day there is even a disembodied voice that perpetually describes the 'ritual of mummification in Ancient Egypt', making a mockery of the secrecy of my forefathers' tradition for all to hear.

Frankly, it's not the kind of immortality I imagined for myself.

But how about you, Moses? How are you bearing up? I hear they worship you as some kind of holy man these days, that you immortalised yourself within the pages of a book, while all your followers argue about the meaning of inscriptions on stone tablets. Perhaps we are not so very different after all, you and I.

I've had a lot of opportunity to reflect on the time that we spent together, as a family, in the early days, before all the unpleasantness. Of course, I always knew that your mother had abandoned you at a very young age, but I tried not to make a big thing of it.

When you had that extraordinary 'conversion', it seemed to give a new form and sense of purpose to everything that was unexpressed. You became some kind of zealot, a thing possessed. There was a time when I superstitiously almost believed that all those cataclysmic signs and wonders were a manifestation of your own fury, but I couldn't imagine how one man could be so angry.

To the end, though, I could never have believed in the message of your faceless 'Supreme God', who had neither animal nor human features. 'Set my people free,' you said. It seemed like anarchy to me; I lived by the edict 'Serve my people'. Surely things can only be well when everyone keeps their correct place in the sacred order? But there's no point in rehearsing old arguments. Not now that many of our descendants are motherless, and fatherless too, fighting in all the lands that we once held dear.

Maybe our feud was too large to be contained in a generation. I feel it all behind the glass, and my memories return to haunt me. Disasters happening and thousands dying again. Kingdoms rising and falling.

And again I am powerless to prevent it.

The darkness of the nights is so long. I begin to sense that perhaps I have failed. Not because I wouldn't submit to a new foreign religion, or because I refused to dismantle my father's empire. No. I sense that I have failed because I couldn't keep peace between brothers in my own family, and for that I am deeply ashamed.

I'm sorry we fought, Moses. Perhaps, over time, you can forgive me.

John Ablett

Are you ready? (Exodus 12:1–4)

A: Are you ready?

B: Stick, sandals, stomach ache … ugh!

A: What a feast, eh? Roast lamb on the hoof!

B: We had goat, and not a mouthful of hoof among it!

A: I always wondered what roasted lamb-lungs tasted like … not bad at all!

B: Haggis by any other name ... yeuch!

A: For once I was glad of our huge family – we scoffed the lot no bother!

B: For once I was glad of our greedy guzzler Joe next door, always sticking his nose in when anybody's cooking. This time I said: 'Have as much as you like Joe, really!'

A: Fast food, it's the in thing and I'm all for it. Uncle Zeb couldn't do his usual and talk the hind legs off a donkey all through dinner!

B: Joe would eat the hind legs off a donkey, that's for sure.

A: I've got a great feeling, you know!

B: I've got a terrible feeling – indigestion!

A: But are you ready?

B: I don't think I've ever been more ready. I'm not going to eat for a week, or a fortnight, or a month. What month is it anyway?

A: It's the first month.

B: The first month of what?

A: The first month of our new futures.

B: I don't think the Egyptians are going to like that.

A: They don't have to like it. We're not going to be around to find out.

B: Do you think the blood on the door will keep us safe?

A: Let's hope so.

   (Pause)

B: Can you hear wailing?

A: It's started. Let's go.

Jo Love, **Spill the Beans**

I am an Israelite. I'm an Egyptian (Exodus 14)

For two voices*

Hello, my name is Chaya. It means 'full of life'. I'm an Israelite. What that means is that I belong to the people of Israel, and our leader is Moses.

Hello, my name is Jabari. It means 'brave'. I'm an Egyptian. I live in the land of Egypt and our leader is Pharaoh.

Our people have lived in Egypt for a long time as slaves to Pharaoh's army. Moses has told us that soon we will go on a long journey and be free.

I am in the Egyptian army. I'm a foot soldier. I carry a shield and a sword. Our army has foot soldiers and spearmen and archers and charioteers who drive the war chariots. One day I might get to drive a chariot too.

There have been plagues in Egypt – the river has turned to blood, there have been gnats and flies, locusts have eaten the crops – there have been frogs – thousands of frogs. Moses has told us that God is sending the plagues on the Egyptians and that Pharaoh will let us go.

It's been awful in Egypt – there has been fire and thunder and darkness, our animals have died of diseases. Last night was the worst – in each of our families the oldest child died. My big brother died. Pharaoh has said Moses is behind this and has ordered all the Israelites to leave our land. They have set off towards the Red Sea. I hate Moses for killing my brother.

My name is Chaya. It means 'full of life'. I'm an Israelite. Listen to what happened to me.

My name is Jabari. It means 'brave'. I'm an Egyptian. Listen to what happened to me too.

We are on the move. We had to pack our things together very quickly. We have taken only the things we can carry. Pharaoh told Moses last night that he is letting us go.

The Israelites have gone. There are rumours that Pharaoh may be about to tell the army to go after them. We are getting ready to move.

Moses is leading us. We are following a special cloud in the daytime and at night there is a fire in the sky. Moses says this is God showing us the way to go.

We are chasing the Israelites. Pharaoh has told us to capture them and bring them back. They are running as fast as they can go. But they have older people and children with them who slow them down. We are Pharaoh's army – we have weapons, we have chariots, we are fit and strong. We can move fast.

People are worried. We can see in the distance that Pharaoh's army is coming after us. If the Egyptian army catches up with us they may kill us. Moses has said that God will look after us, that God will fight for us. I'm scared.

We are getting nearer. We can see the Israelites in the far distance. We will catch up with them soon.

Some of our leaders are telling Moses that we should have stayed in Egypt – that it would have been better to stay as slaves in Egypt than to die here in the wilderness. Many of the children are tired and hungry. Some of them are crying.

We are getting near to the Red Sea. I can smell the salt in the air. Soon the Israelites will have to stop. There will be nowhere for them to go.

We have reached the sea. Moses has called us all together and told us that the Lord our God will fight for us today. We have no weapons. How can God save us? I don't understand.

The Israelites don't seem to be moving. They have stopped at the seashore. Tomorrow we will catch up with them and fight. We are getting prepared for battle. My sword is sharp and bright. I am ready.

Something amazing has happened. Moses stretched out his hand and God sent a wind across the sea all night and it blew back the waves and formed a dry path through the sea. We are walking through the sea on dry ground in the middle of the night. The waves are like huge water walls either side of us and we are dry!

The Israelites are getting away – the sea seems to have rolled back into a dry path – we are going after them. They will not escape.

We are still walking through the sea but Pharaoh's army are coming after us. We are all frightened but Moses has said that God is in charge.

Something is happening to the seabed. Our chariot wheels are getting clogged up. It's getting harder to move. Our captain has just told us that we are going to turn back. He says that the Israelites' God is fighting for them and we cannot win.

We have stopped again – in the middle of the sea – it is nearly dawn. Moses has stretched out his hand and behind us the sea is rolling back. Pharaoh's army have turned back – they are racing through the returning waves.

The water is coming back. We are racing for the shore. We have abandoned the chariots. They are stuck. They will not move. I have left my shield behind but I still have my sword. We are running for our lives.

It is over! The whole of Pharaoh's army is dead. They drowned before they could reach the shore. We will never see them again. We have crossed the Red Sea. We are all safe on dry land.

My name was Jabari. I was an Egyptian. I was a foot soldier in Pharaoh's army. I was drowned in the Red Sea. I was brave.

My name is Chaya. I am an Israelite. I am 'full of life'. Moses is our leader. Tomorrow we will journey on.

Ruth Burgess

* Note: Chaya is a female name. This script could be read by a woman and a man or by older children.

Running, running (Exodus 14)

We are standing on the seashore.

We are the Israelites. We are running – running.
Pharaoh's army are after us. They are coming – coming.

Moses, our leader, says – God will be with us.

**We are the Israelites. We are running – running.
Pharaoh's army are after us. They are coming – coming.**

God sent a wind that blew all night.

**We are the Israelites. We are running – running.
Pharaoh's army are after us . They are coming – coming.**

The wind blew the waves of the sea right back.

**We are the Israelites. We are running – running.
Pharaoh's army are after us. They are coming – coming.**

There is a road going through the sea.

**We are the Israelites. We are running – running.
Pharaoh's army are after us. They are coming – coming.**

There are walls of water up the sides of the road.

**We are the Israelites. We are running – running.
Pharaoh's army are after us. They are coming – coming.**

We are walking on the road right through the sea.

**We are the Israelites. We are running – running.
Pharaoh's army are after us. They are coming – coming.**

We have reached dry land and the waves are rolling back.

**We are the Israelites. We are running – running.
Pharaoh's army are after us. They are coming – coming.**

The sea has rolled back.
Pharaoh's army have drowned.
They've stopped coming.

We're resting now and we've stopped … **running.**

Ruth Burgess

The survivor's wife (Exodus 14:23–31)

Let me make one thing clear at the start.
My husband is a good man;
I am fond of him.
Yes, I know he spends more money on beer than I would like and
he loses money in gambling.
But he is never violent to me or the children;
there's always enough money left for food and clothes,
just.
So I am glad he was spared.
I am delighted that his chariot lost a wheel
so he didn't make it to the Red Sea.
But many other good men,
possibly better men,
did.
They drowned.
And those wretched escaped slaves rejoiced,
celebrated.
So if there is one deity
or many,
there are two questions I would like to ask:
Why was he spared?
Neither he nor I are overly pious,
particularly righteous.
And why, surrounded by grieving friends and colleagues,
do we feel guilty?

Brian Ford

Not counting (Exodus 15:19–21)

They were tired:
tired of cajoling the children,
tired of packing and unpacking and packing,
tired of carrying the food and the cooking pans,
tired of walking.

I didn't think that they had any energy left,
but they did.

They were anxious:
anxious about their enemies,
anxious about their older ones and their little ones,
anxious about the future,
anxious about the unknown.

I didn't think that they could let go of their anxieties, even for a moment,
but they could.
It was a risk.
I thought I might be on my own,
that no one would join me,
that I'd look a fool.

I wondered if, after my brother's long song,
my sisters would have had enough of singing,
but they hadn't.

And so I sang for them,
and I sang with them
and I danced
and I played my tambourine.

And the dry ground was beaten firm
by the feet of six hundred thousand women dancing,
not counting men,
and sheep and goats and cattle,
and children.

Ruth Burgess

Enough – simply enough (Exodus 16)

Enough – simply enough,
not too much,
not an overabundance,
but – enough.

Sufficient for the day,
not for storing up
or hoarding for the lean times,
but – enough.

Seems fair that everyone
should get just what they need
regardless of status,
just – enough.

These are the resources
supplied by God.

Liz Crumlish, Spill the Beans

Miriam and Mary (Exodus 16)

Well, Miriam.
Well, Mary.
We did it, Miriam.
Yes, we did it, Mary.
They said we'd never do it, Miriam.
But we did do it, Mary.
And we did it well, Miriam.
We sure did. Mary, we sure did.

It took us ages, Miriam.
But we had ages, Mary.
All that persuading, Miriam.
All that collecting, Mary.
All that writing down, Miriam.

All those parchment pages, Mary.
But we did it, Miriam.
Yes, we did it, Mary.

Do you remember how it started, Miriam?
I do, Mary.
We'd told Moses that we were hungry, Miriam.
And he'd told God that we were hungry, Mary.
And God sorted it, Miriam.
God definitely sorted it, Mary.
Quails for dinner, Miriam.
And manna for breakfast and lunch, Mary.

It took us a while to get used to it, Miriam.
It sure did, Mary.
Especially the manna, Miriam.
Especially the manna, Mary.
And if you gathered too much manna, Miriam.
It wasn't very nice, Mary.
All those worms, Miriam.
And the smell, Mary.
But the manna was good, Miriam.
Sweet as honey, Mary.
And the quails tasted good, Miriam.
Very good, Mary.
But after a week of quails and manna, Miriam.
It got very boring, Mary.
And then Moses told us, Miriam.
It was quails and manna for forty years, Mary!

It was then we had our great idea, Miriam.
We sure did, Mary.
We called all the women together, Miriam.
Every single one of them, Mary.
And we told them about our great idea, Miriam.
And they thought it was a grand idea, Mary.
And they all said they'd help, Miriam.
And they did, Mary.

They brought us their ideas, Miriam.
And such ideas, Mary.
Some simple ideas, Miriam.
And some very complicated ones, Mary.
Some brilliant ideas, Miriam.
And some crazy ideas, Mary.
And we wrote them all down, Miriam.
We sure did, Mary.
There was manna à la locust, Miriam.
And quail au vin, Mary.
There was manna roly-poly, Miriam.
And quail low-fat haggis, Mary.
There was manna crumble, Miriam.
And stuffed quail pasties, Mary.
And we had to try them all out, Miriam.
It was hard hard work, Mary.

Well, Miriam.
Well, Mary.
We finally got it finished, Miriam.
We did, Mary.
And here it is, Miriam.
It's beautiful, Mary.
Bound in a scroll, Miriam.
It was worth the effort, Mary.

And we're going to ask Moses, Miriam.
And Aaron too, Mary.
If they'll put it with the jar of manna, Miriam.
In front of the covenant box, Mary.
So that our descendants can read it, Miriam.
The fruit of our labours, Mary.
The Wilderness Cookery Book, Miriam.
Our Wilderness Cookery Book, Mary.

The Wilderness Cookery Book, by Mary and Miriam (said together).

Ruth Burgess

Water from a rock (Exodus 17:1–7)

Use 2 female voices.

A: Water's off again!

B: What? You're having a laugh!

A: I wish I was, but we're all unpacked, the tent is up, and then Joe says to me, 'Oh, by the way, there's no water.'

B: It's that Moses again, isn't it? He is hopeless. And that Aaron isn't much better. They spend too much time looking up and not enough time looking down, thinking about us!

A: I hear you, and I'm filthy … look at me. The dirty clothes are piled up, and what am I supposed to do?

B: Oh, and that poor wee girl who's due any day now. We have the towels but no water. What good is that?

A: And the weans are going to start screaming that they're thirsty, just you wait.

B: We won't get an hour of sleep.

A: Worst of all is that I can't blame them.

B: Aye, I could murder a nice cool drink right about now.

A: My tongue is sticking to the top of my mouth like I've been eating too many of yon Jacob's crackers.

B: So, what are we going to do about it?

A: It usually comes down to us, doesn't it? As long as the jugs are full of water and there is food on the table, then the menfolk don't even think about where it comes from.

B: Well, just like usual, we're going to have to go walking miles to find the nearest spring or see if there is a well around here somewhere.

A: It's just bad planning, isn't it?

B: We'd do things differently if we were in charge.

A: Oh dear, I'm really starting to feel parched now. We'd better see what we can find.

B: Wait a minute, do you hear that?

A: Hear what?

B: Listen to that rabble shouting and cheering; they won't be so merry when they realise the skins are all empty.

A: Did they just say they had found water? From a rock?

B: God be praised, so they did!

Spill the Beans

The sort of God they preferred (Exodus 32:1–14)

Moses always felt he was walking on eggshells. You know that way of balancing between two sides who don't seem to get on with each other? That's what Moses felt he was doing – every day.

Moses didn't like being in the middle of it. So it was a bit of a relief for him to be called up the mountain to be in God's presence, leaving the people down below.

But no sooner had he gone when the people of Israel started complaining again. 'Where's he gone?' … 'Why has he gone up there and left us down here?' … 'When will he be back?' … And like typical teenagers they took the time out to their advantage and chose to rewrite the rules a little.

It didn't take long for them to persuade Aaron to back their plan of designing a new god – one they could see, one that looked like a god, and that was worth something. So they took all the gold rings they had and melted them all together, and cast them into a statue of a golden calf.

This was the sort of god they preferred. He didn't have them wandering around the desert not knowing where they were going. They took the golden calf with them. They were in charge once more. And so they feasted at the altar of the golden calf.

The Almighty, however, had been keeping an eye on their doings down below the mountain, and Moses rolled his eyes when God, in fury, described what had been going on while Moses was away:

'Look at those stubborn, hard-headed people! What shall I do with them? I free them from slavery, I feed them in the desert, I find water for them, I promise them a new home – and what do they do to return my love? They find another god to follow! I can't stand it any longer! Get back down there, Moses, because I've had enough. This is the last time they turn their backs on me. Do they not know what's good for them?!'

Moses whispered under his breath that no, they didn't know what was good for them, and found himself on those eggshells once more:

'Look, God, you know how it is. They just need a little more time to get used to the idea that you are not out to get them. You led them out into a desert and they thought they were going to die but you saved them. Is that all a waste? They were thirsty and couldn't find fresh water and you supplied it. You don't regret that, do you? They are just growing up. Their theological hormones haven't settled down yet. They are having to rewrite their whole history and belief system and it is taking time. Think of Abraham to whom you promised a new land and many generations' …

And God went silent, and Moses left the mountain to let God think it over once more.

Spill the Beans

Special places (Exodus 33:7–11)

Jessie had a special place that she loved to go to. It was a quiet place high up on the moor above her house. It was by a stream. It took Jessie about forty minutes to get from her home to her special place. She sometimes stayed there for hours, listening to the birds and watching the water bubble down the hillside. Sometimes Jessie took a friend with her to her special place. Sometimes she went alone. If you were to ask Jessie why she loved her special place on the moors, she would probably tell you that she loved the quiet, and she had found that it was a good place to sit and think.

David and Michael had a special place. It was in their house, behind the sofa in the front room. They kept some of their toys there. As long as they didn't leave a mess mum didn't seem to mind them playing there. It was a great place to play on a wet day.

Claire's family always went to the same place for their holiday. It was a house at the seaside. Claire could remember playing on the sands when she was tiny. She and her brother enjoyed looking for crabs in the sea pools. Her mum liked sitting on the sands with a book and sometimes helped them make a sandcastle. Her dad often took her and her brother for a walk or to play golf on the dunes. Claire's family always went to the same place for their holiday – it was their special place.

Some of the people in the Bible had special places. Moses sometimes talked to God in a tent or on a mountain. Women often met together at the side of a well. Elijah once slept in a quiet cave.

Maybe you've got a special place where you and your family like to go together?

Ruth Burgess, Spill the Beans

The encounter (Exodus 33:7–11, 34:29)

I step forward
towards the place where we will meet.
Sand wraps my feet.
I am drawn by the gentlest of threads.
With each step I stand taller.
I am content with who and what I am.
My heartbeat slows.
A tear of expectation is dried quickly by the sun.
The silence grows.
My friend greets me.
The softest of hands.
The softest of voices.
All is heard.
Nothing is left unsaid between us.
As I return my face glows.

Ann Jepson

That shine (Exodus 34:29–35)

(A dialogue between mother and child)

Mum, who's that man?

He's a special man, dear.

Why is he special, mum?

Because he's our leader, love.

What's his name, mum? Is that special too?

All our names are special, you know that. His name is Moses.

Why is he called Moses, mum? It's a funny name.

Because he was given his name by an Egyptian princess, love.

So he's a prince, mum?

No, dear. He's an Israelite, like us. But he is our leader.

He's been away a long time, mum. Where's he been?

He went up into the mountain, love, to meet with God.

Why did he come back down with those lumps of stone, mum? They must be very heavy.

They've got writing on them, dear. Moses says they are laws and he's going to read them to us.

Can I be there when he does it, mum?

No, love, it'll be past your bedtime and you'd fall asleep while he was reading.

I wouldn't, mum, I promise. I'd stay wide awake and be watching him all the time.

But why would you want to do that, dear? It's mainly for grown-ups.

Aw, mum! Please!

I'll never understand you, child. Why do you want to be there?

I want to see how long it takes to get that shine off his face.

Shine off his face …? But, why?

Because I want to know how long the shine lasts when somebody has been talking to God.

Marjorie Dobson

Leviticus

Holy and just (Leviticus 19)

Be holy.
Don't harvest your fields to the edges.
Don't gather the grapes you missed on first picking.
Leave some food for those who need it.
Be holy in the land.

Be holy.
Don't steal or cheat or lie.
Don't keep back anyone's wages.
Use honest scales and measures.
Be holy in the marketplace.

Be holy.
Don't bear grudges, sort out your differences.
Don't favour the rich over the poor.
Speak up for those who seek justice.
Be holy in the courts.

Be holy.
Don't take advantage of those with disabilities.
Don't spread lies.
Show respect for older people.
Be holy in your lives.

Be holy.
Be honest.
Keep your promises.
Love your neighbour.
Love your neighbour as much as you love yourself.

Be holy.
Be honest.
Be generous.
Be loving.
Be holy in the land.

Ruth Burgess

You shall not reap to the very edges (Leviticus 19:9–10)

When you reap the harvest of your land, you shall not reap to the very edges of your field, or gather the gleanings of your harvest. You shall not strip your vineyard bare, or gather the fallen grapes: you shall leave them for the poor and the alien: I am the Lord your God (Lev 19:9–10, NRSV).

When we stock
more food than
we will ever
eat
rather than sharing
with the hungry,
we glean what little
hope
remains for others,
leaving their hearts as
empty
as their stomachs.

Thom M Shuman

Any of your kin (Leviticus 25:35)

If any of your kin fall into difficulty and become dependent on you, you shall support them; they shall live with you as though resident aliens (Lev 25:35, NRSV).

If the family from
Aleppo
are my cousins,
if the immigrant
mum
working three jobs
is my sister,
if the Muslim
teenager
is my son,
if the hungry
girl
is my daughter,
how
can I turn
my back on
any
(or all)
of them?

Thom M Shuman

Numbers

A blessing on and a blessing from (Numbers 6:24–26)

Dear Ruth,

I read your recent request for reflections on Old Testament verses and my mind went back to my boarding school days over 70 years ago. A Bible text was recited before breakfast every morning. I have the list to this day. My favourite verses are from the Book of Numbers.

After my husband died, the time came to think of the wording to put on his headstone. Following his name and dates we added 'Tea Planter' to reflect his fulfilled working years in India and Central Africa. Across the lower part of the stone we returned to a much loved text and added the words 'The Lord bless thee and keep thee'.

This was to be a blessing both on him and also from him on anyone who might pause to read his inscription as they passed by.

Deirdre Hearn

He beat me (Numbers 22:21–35)

He beat me
not once
but three times.

He was angry
I would not go
where he wanted me to go
and he beat me.

He was mad
and I crushed his foot
against a wall
and he beat me.

He was raging
and I lay down in front of him
and refused to get up
and he beat me.

And then he saw
what I could see:
he saw the angel.

I'd never seen an angel before
and I never saw one again,
but I am happy to remember
that an angel of God
once challenged the foolishness of a human being
and defended the wisdom of a donkey.

Ruth Burgess

Deuteronomy

The best of your heart (Deuteronomy 4:31)

Because the Lord your God is a merciful God, he will neither abandon you nor destroy you; he will not forget the covenant with your ancestors that he swore to them (Deut 4:31, NRSV).

When we long
to walk away,
you trail behind,
refusing to take the hint;

when we offer you the
worst of our souls, you
continue to give us
the best of your
heart.

Thom M Shuman

Ten obligations, ten commandments (Deuteronomy 5:1–21)

Ten obligations, ten commandments – how many can you remember?

Loads.

Go on then.

Don't steal, don't murder, don't commit adultery – everyone remembers that one.

Keep going.

Don't tell lies about your neighbour and don't covet what's not yours – how many's that?

Five.

OK – look after your parents, pay them respect – that's six, and have a rest on Sundays – that's seven …

Three to go.

Don't kill?

You've had that one – it's the same as don't murder.

Don't swear?

It actually says don't take God's name in vain, but don't swear will do – two to go …

Errrr?

Yes?

I'm stuck.

Want some help?

Please.

I am the Lord your God who brought you out of …

Egypt.

You shall have no other gods …

But me! Phew! Is that it?

One more – last one.

No idea.

Clue: Aaron made one of these.

Who's Aaron?

Moses' brother.

Aaron made a golden one of these.

Did he?

OK – more help – Aaron made a golden idol. And one of the commandments was – don't make ...

Idols?

Correct!

Ten commandments. How many can you remember?

Ruth Burgess

Learning the rules (Deuteronomy 5:1–21)

Annie's big sister was learning how to drive.

'Is it hard?' asked Annie.

'Well,' said Sally, 'bits of it are hard – there's lots of rules to learn.'

'What kind of rules?' asked Annie.

'Rules about the road,' said Sally. 'Rules that keep everyone safe. I'll ask you a couple of questions – see if you know the answers ... Here's one: you are driving along a country road. A horse and rider are approaching. What should you do? Mark two answers: Rev your engine. Flash your headlights. Give plenty of room. Sound your horn. Drive slowly past. Increase your speed.'

'Ummm,' said Annie. 'I think you should give them plenty of room and ... and drive past very slowly so that you don't frighten the horse.'

'Well done,' said Sally. 'One more?'

'OK,' said Annie.

'What is the safest way to use a mobile phone in your vehicle? Mark one answer: Use hands-free equipment. Drive slowly on a quiet road. Direct your call through the operator. Find a suitable place to stop.'

'Ummm,' said Annie. 'Well, a hands-free phone is good but probably finding a safe place to stop is better.'

'Well done,' said Sally. 'You're good at this and only 6 years to go and you can take your own driving test.'

Annie laughed. Six years was a long long time.

You could talk about other rules that help to keep people safe, at home … in school … in the car … on the train …

Ruth Burgess, Spill the Beans

Hope for a better tomorrow (Deuteronomy 24:20)

And the dove returned to Noah in the evening, and in her mouth was an olive leaf plucked from the tree …

You give us hope,
olive leaf
olive fruit
olive tree,
hope for a better tomorrow.

You give us oil to make us cheerful
oil for light
oil for strength
oil for anointing.

You give us wood from the land
wood to burn
wood to carve
wood to build.

You give us leaves of green and silver
leaves of growth
leaves of new life
leaves of beauty.

You give us a harvest of green and black olives
olives for health
olives to share
olives for food.

You give us hope,
olive leaf
olive fruit
olive tree,
you give us light and strength and healing.

You give us hope for a better tomorrow.

When you beat your olive tree, do not go over the branches again, its fruit shall be for the migrant and the stranger and for those who need it.

Ruth Burgess

Making the harvest offering (Deuteronomy 26)

Caleb comes in and meets Helek, Simeon, Joseph and Asher. They are all carrying baskets with their harvest offerings. Three children, Rachel, Nathan and Hannah, are tagging along.

Caleb: God be with you, neighbours.

Helek: And with you, neighbour Caleb. You look happy. Are you going to have a good harvest?

Caleb: Not bad at all. It looks like a good year for grapes.

Helek: And my olives have given a really good crop this time.

Simeon: My bees have given me plenty of honey.

Joseph: I've done well with my figs.

Asher: And the barley harvest will be good too. There will be plenty to eat for everyone this winter. God is good.

Rachel: Daddy, why are you all carrying those baskets?

Caleb: That's a very good question. We're going to the Temple to give God the first fruits of our harvest.

Rachel: Is that what you've got in your baskets?

Helek: That's right. Look, I've got some of my best olives.

Simeon: And I've brought the first pot of my honey. And the first cabbage from my garden.

Rachel: But why are you taking them to the Temple?

Caleb: Because the Bible tells us to.

Joseph: That's what it says in the book of God's Law. 'After you have gone into the land that the Lord your God is giving you, and have settled there, each of you must take the first part of every crop that you harvest, and put it in a basket, and take it to the Temple.'

Nathan: What do you do with it when you get there?

Asher: We give it to the priest who's on duty.

Hannah: Aren't there some special words you have to say?

Asher: Yes. God's Law says, 'Go to the priest in charge at that time, and say to him, "I now acknowledge to the Lord my God that I have entered the land which he promised our ancestors to give us" …'

Helek: 'Then, in the Lord's presence, you will recite these words …'

Simeon: 'My ancestor was a wandering Aramean, who took his family to live in Egypt.'

Caleb: 'They were few in number when they went there, but they became a large and powerful nation.'

Joseph: 'The Egyptians treated us harshly, and forced us to work as slaves.'

Asher: 'Then we cried out for help to the Lord, the God of our ancestors.'

Helek: 'He heard us and saw our hardship, suffering and misery.'

Simeon: 'By his great power and strength he rescued us from Egypt.'

Caleb: 'He worked miracles and wonders, and caused terrifying things to happen.'

Joseph:	'He brought us here, and gave us this rich and fertile land.'
Asher:	'So now I bring to the Lord the first part of the harvest that he has given me.'
Rachel:	And you have to say *all* those words *every time*?
Nathan:	Every year. And when I'm a man I shall say them too. But you won't – because you're only a girl.
Rachel:	Nyaah!
Hannah:	We get to cook the food for the party. And if you're mean – you won't get any!
Rachel:	What do you do, after you've finished saying the words?
Helek:	Then we set our baskets down in the Lord's presence and worship him.
Joseph:	We have to be grateful for all the good things the Lord has given to us and to our families.
Rachel:	And then?
Caleb:	Then we have the party. Is all the food ready?
Hannah:	Nearly. Mother just sent me and Rachel out to fetch some more apples for the apple-cakes.
Rachel:	And Nathan tagged along with us, but he can't help with the cooking – because he's only a boy!
Nathan:	I shall go along to the Temple and learn all the things I have to do when I'm a man.
Asher:	Come on then – in peace! This is the Lord's harvest celebration, and we need to be friends with one another during the feast.

Liz Varley

Choices (Deuteronomy 30:15)

See I have set before you today life and prosperity, death and adversity (Deut 30:15).

Get up now or snuggle in?
Toast, cereal, tea or coffee?
Zesty lemon shower gel or honey and almond?
Blue socks or green?
Shoes or boots?
Walk or drive?

From the minute we open our eyes
or not
our day is full of choices.
Some huge, some little
but all with consequences.
Impacting us and our neighbour,
folk like us with choices
and folk for whom there are no options
only unremitting sameness
and resignation.

So whether the deal
seems big or small
whatever the ease or difficulty of decision
may we always value the luxury of choice
and may our choices be life-enhancing.

Liz Crumlish

On Mount Nebo (Deuteronomy 34:1–12)

A dialogue between Moses and Joshua, as though up on Mount Nebo. Moses needs to wear a robe or suchlike, under which is hidden a relay baton.

Moses: Well, would you look at this! We've actually made it. We're back.

Joshua: Bit of a roundabout route, but what's forty years, eh!

Moses: Erm, four hundred and some, more like.

Joshua: Did it feel that long?!

Moses: No, I mean that's how long we've really been gone. Before Egypt, before Pharaoh, before slavery, this was our home! And we're finally back.

Joshua: Is that what kept you going? Imagining this place?

Moses: Ha! Let me tell you, I needed a lot more than that to get me to get you lot here. But yes, I did imagine this place …

Joshua: Can you see Abraham's old house from here?

Moses: Oh, ya daftie. How would I know? I'm not that old!

Joshua: We should find it though, and open it up as a museum! After all that digging we did in the desert, we'll be great at unearthing archaeological finds! Abraham's crook, Jacob's old soup pots, Esau's bow and arrow, the complete heritage centre. We can bury you there, too, with a plaque. And should we plant you an oak tree?

Moses: Joshua, we're not here to build shrines to the past. *(Wistfully, and almost to himself)* And you'll have more important things to do …

Joshua: But what you've achieved should stand for all time! People should know!

Moses: What people should know is that we got here together. I needed Zuar's encouragement and Elishama's wisdom. I needed Adina's shoulder to cry on – and Ofra's hot dinners! Whatever's been achieved, it's taken all of us.

Joshua: No, your part has outshone everyone's!

Moses: No, my part was I happened to pay attention to a burning bush. Many's the time I've wished I'd ignored it! The rest has been about all of us, together or not at all. Think about it. What's kept you going? Putting me on a pedestal – or your mother's stew and your cousins' games and Rina's prayer times and Joab teaching you to be a man?! …

Joshua: (after a pause, nodding slowly and chuckling) OK, I see what you mean … you're right! But what have I done, what has my part been?

Moses: You know how a relay race goes, Joshua?

Joshua: (puzzled) Uh-uh …?

Moses: (revealing the relay baton and holding it out to Joshua) It's your turn now. Trust God. Keep the vision alive.

Joshua looks at the relay baton, takes it firmly and looks back at Moses. They hold each other's gaze.

Jo Love, **Spill the Beans**

Joshua

Rahab (Joshua 2:1–21)

For this mission, we were chosen –
fastest runners of a quick-paced people
with a history of backdoor exits.

It was our God who sent us to witness
the promised land, the land of staying.
And it was our God, ways oblique,

who sent us this woman
with chambers scented of intimacy
when our enemies hunted us as spies and dogs.

We did not see her bed but her roof, with clean flax
for cover. Through our worry we remembered
the Egyptian farms our parents worked in the dark ages

when our people did not yet fear daylight,
our daily faults hidden
by the oppressors' transgressions.

After the soldiers of Jericho left, Rahab watched the lamps
of her city and told us tales of our God: havoc and love.
Her words were steadier than our holiest invocations.

When we returned to camp we were the same
and not the same. In the desert, we have only our histories,
repeated fierce through generations. Scrabbling for truth

in each other is hard: looking at our fiery God
makes us a little mad. Sand numerous
as crowds. In a city, staying put, faith might be as simple

as a scarlet thread hanging in the window
as the shouts of our army draw near.

Cara Bertron

Gossip about spies (Joshua 2:1–24)

And what were they doing in a place like that,
may I ask?
Two good Jewish boys,
they had a job to do.

I can guess:
day's work done –
time for some fun.
Well, they very nearly paid very dearly for it,
didn't they?

And what right had they to promise
that she and her household would be saved?
And Joshua agreed!
And some of our boys had to be diverted
from their Yahweh-given duties
to take care of them.

What kind of religion saves whores?
Eh?

Brian Ford

No going back (Joshua 3:7–17)

A pensive but deeply hopeful monologue by Joshua

Getting out of the place that has held you captive …
entering into the place you truly belong …
either way, there's always a crossing over.
And when the sea opens up before you
and closes in behind you,
there's no going back.

And the question is always:
what's on the other side?

Will the grass really be any greener?
Should you not just stay put with the devils you know?
Moses led us from Egypt.
I had to lead us from the wilderness.
Two merciless places, but they were home;
the only home ever known, to those leaving them behind.
But when the sea opens up before you
and closes in behind you,
there's no going back.

We were still captives in the wilderness;
captives to our fears, our immaturity, our victim mentality.
Some of the whingeing voices were only silenced by death.
We learned the hard way about refusing to grow up and move on.
But when the sea opens up before you
and closes in behind you,
there's no going back.

So, from a burning bush or a flooding river …
different starting places, different paths ahead,
but for both of us,
yes, a crossing over from where we've reached
to where we need to go next.
And when the sea opens up before you
and closes in behind you,
there's no going back.

Welcome home! … to this strange land,
where everything has changed
and yet God is still with us.
For the sea opened up before us
and closed in behind us,
and, may God be praised,
there's no going back!

Jo Love, Spill the Beans

Crossing over with wellington boots (Joshua 3)

One of the boldest stories in the Old Testament is that of Joshua leading the Israelites across the River Jordan and into Jericho.

The people follow the priests, who are carrying the Ark of the Covenant, into the River Jordan. The waters roll back and the people cross safely to the other side.

How would we have felt if we'd been asked to pack up our tents, follow Joshua's command and take a path that is set right through the middle of the River Jordan in full flood? Would we have been able to trust that this was the right way to go?

Up and down the country, old chapels and small churches are having to close down. Church communities are having to pack up, move on and start afresh in an unfamiliar building with a community they may not know. This causes some folk to feel quite bereft as long-cherished patterns of life come to an end. Others are excited at the opportunities of a new challenge.

In our town of Poole a vision of transformation arose encouraging all five Methodist churches to move together to become one membership. The focus was to redevelop the largest of the churches, right in the middle of Poole High Street where hundreds of shoppers pass every day, and to develop a community of local charities that would work independently alongside the church.

We eventually reached the point where we needed to make the last move into the high-street building. Some members were bubbling with excitement – they had waited so long for this moment. Others were understandably clinging to the pews they'd known for so long, and were worried about details like parking.

So, one morning our minister preached on this text from Joshua, pointing out that God had gone before us: the leaders had consulted and prayed for clarity, pastoral care had been given, everyone was included in the decision, and we were taking ancient treasures from each church with us. God had been with us in Poole all through our long history and wasn't going to let us down now.

The question was asked: *'If I put my wellington boots on and go down to the riverbank and stand on the path, will you come with me: will you put on your boots and cross over into the new future that God has for us? Will you fulfil the promise we made when we started: to go into the future as one community, in faith? ... Please stand if you're willing to make the crossing.'*

One by one the people stood, until we all were standing.

A few weeks later, we adopted as our temporary logo a pair of wellington boots!

Tricia Creamer

The scarlet cord (Joshua 6:15–25)

Am I mad? Is this piece of cord really going to save me and those I love?

I knew those lodgers were probably spies: they asked too many questions. Yet when I heard that the king's guard was searching for them, I couldn't turn them in. It wasn't just because I'd heard the rumours about the Israelites: how they'd completely destroyed the Amorites on the other side of the river, and how their God had promised them our land; there was something about those men – something I couldn't quite put my finger on – that told me it was true. They had a confidence which wasn't arrogance. That's why when I helped them escape, I asked them to spare me and my family. They agreed. All I had to do was tie a scarlet cord in my window.

That was almost two weeks ago. I've had all the family staying with me ever since. This last week, the Israelites have been marching round the city each day with trumpets blaring.

Is this piece of cord really going to save us? Perhaps I should pray to their God? ...

Angie Allport

Judges

Birth of Samson (Judges 13)

Wife: Manoah! Manoah! I've something to tell you …

Manoah: What is it, dear?

Wife: We're going to have a son!

Manoah: In your dreams! After all this time – I don't believe it.

Wife: It's true – I had a message from God.

Manoah: Now I know you're dreaming! Why would God send a message to you and not me?

Wife: It wasn't a dream! There was this gorgeous young man – just like an angel – and he gave me this message.

Manoah: You're sure that's not all he gave you?

Wife: Don't be so crude! This was a message from God.

Manoah: All right then – so what did he say?

Wife: I'm not to drink any alcohol, and to eat only clean food till he's born. Then he's going to be dedicated to God as a Nazirite, and he's going to save us from our enemies.

Manoah: It all sounds a bit far-fetched to me! And the only time I've known you to give up alcohol it only lasted a week!

Wife: Well, you can talk! The way you emptied that last bottle of wine.

Manoah: Well, it all sounds a bit far-fetched to me! I won't believe it till I hear it for myself. If God's really got a message for us why wouldn't he give it directly to me – after all, I am the man of the family!

***

Enter wife, with messenger

Wife: Manoah! Manoah! Come quickly – he's here again!

Manoah: *(running towards her, panting)* OK, OK, I'm coming … So who on earth are you? And what are you doing with my wife? What's all this about?

Messenger: I've already told your wife – she's to do just as I said. No alcohol, no impure foods …

Manoah: What are you, a dietician? I don't know what to make of all this! At least tell me your name – and stay and have something to eat with us.

Messenger: I can't stop – and I can't tell you anything about myself – except that it's just as your wife has already told you: I bring a message from God *(leaves).*

Manoah: Well, this God moves in mysterious ways! You mean, we've seen him, and lived to tell the tale?

Wife: I told you – God has a plan for us. You wait and see – in the meantime, I'm going to empty out the wine bottles! *(Wife leaves.)*

Manoah: Hang on a minute, you can't do that – it's only you that's got to stop drinking – women! *(He runs after her.)*

Jan Berry

Boasting in Gaza (Judges 16)

I can still hardly believe that it actually worked;
I really didn't think he could be that stupid.
Four times she asks him to tell her the secret of his strength.
Three times he spins her a yarn.
Three times she believes him,
and he publicly humiliates her,
and the fourth time (can you believe it?)
he tells her the truth.
A quick head shave while he's asleep
and it's out with his eyes and on with the manacles.
All those old clichés about 'strong in the arm, weak in the head'
seem to be true.
They say he was a judge of Israel:
he wasn't much of a judge of character, was he?
He acted like a donkey,
let's treat him like one,
set him to work grinding corn.
By the way,
I have heard that some ultra-cautious, timid simpleton
has suggested that we keep his head shaved.
Don't bother, keep him scruffy.
We've removed a metre's length of dreadlocks,
a bit of stubble isn't going to hurt us,
is it?

Brian Ford

Ruth

Returning (Ruth 1)

1.

Beloveds, once there was hunger
in Bethlehem. Practical tall Elimelech
set out from that place – took one sweet wife Naomi,
two crack-voice sons, four empty bellies,
went to Moab: border-crossers.

Beloveds, soon Elimelech in his tallness died: life
went on. Two sons grew into two men, married two
foreign women in singing Moabite spring. Naomi wept
for her dead husband twice a week; otherwise
they were happy. Then the sons died.

Beloveds, what could the living do? Three women,
three red-eyed salty women! One day, between morning
and noon grief, Naomi heard the Lord had placed bread
on Bethlehem's table. Remembered her friends, the sound
of gossip in her own language, the smell of the olive evening wind.
I shall return, she said, and stepped
out the door. Her face towards her own country.

2.

She and her daughters-in-law went on their way to return
to Bethlehem, in the land of Judah. Orpah, Ruth, Naomi –
only six syllables and one donkey between them. Homing pigeons
wheeling overhead, the desert listening for each next step.

3.

They stopped. Love and tarnation, said Naomi, return
to your mothers' houses and get married again, seize
a chance at happiness spoken in your own tongue.
She kissed them and turned away.

4.

Orpah and Ruth spoke, stumbling in Hebrew,
No, we will return with you to your people.

5.

Willickers and heaven's crumbs, said Naomi to those foolish girls.
Return to your people. I have nothing left for you,
no sons for you to marry. I am old. Go your own way, chickadees.

6.

Naomi continues: Buzzards and shaky bridges, return!
My daughters, it has been far more bitter for me than for you:
the hand of the Lord has turned against me.

Orpah left, but wiry Ruth wrapped her stubborn arms around Naomi.

7.

Naomi: See, your sister-in-law has returned to her people.

8.

Return after your sister-in-law! (This a command from sweet steely
Naomi, Naomi with nothing but her will.)

9.

Ruth's speech: Come hell or high water, I will not return
from following you. If your God is not willing –
I will make your God my God and swear by our God;
if the creek rises, I will find us a boat. Duct tape
and baling wire, I'm bound to you, Naomi, you
and your people and your God. I shall walk where you walk,
sleep where you sleep, be buried where you are buried.
Horsefeathers and holy certainty, may the Hebrews' Yahweh,
may my Yahweh, do thus and so to me, and more as well,
if even death parts me from you.

10.

So Naomi returned to Bethlehem
at the beginning of the barley harvest.

11.

And Ruth the Moabite returned with her to Bethlehem.

Cara Bertron

Ruth and Naomi (Ruth I)

Narrator: Long ago in the days before Israel had a king, three women set out on a long journey … Day one:

Ruth: It was hard to say goodbye to my family, not knowing if I'd ever see them again. My mother cried and my father held me for a long time and I felt his sadness. I know so little about the land to which I'm travelling. It was hard to walk away from all that is familiar to me, all that has been my home. I'm glad that Orpah, my sister-in-law, is coming with us, because we share the same memories, the same stories. We can help each other along.

Narrator: Day two:

Naomi: To be going home was all I ever dreamed of. Ten years in Moab felt like a lifetime. I only went there because Elimelech decided that living and working in a foreign land was better than starving in our own village. But Elimelech is dead and both of my sons died in Moab. I am nothing now; a widow without sons has no identity, no protection. My God has deserted me and left me bitter and alone. There was nothing to keep me in Moab, and they say that the harvest will be good this year in Bethlehem. I still have relatives there and I hope they'll help me. My daughters-in-law, Orpah and Ruth, are coming with me and I'm going home.

Narrator: Day three:

Ruth: Orpah went back to Moab today, back to her home and family. Naomi told her that it made more sense for her to remarry and raise a family in her own community. It was a hard parting. Orpah loved Naomi. We were all in tears. I can't explain why, but I've decided to stay with Naomi. I held on to her and told her that I was going with her. I left no room for argument. We are travelling on.

Narrator: Day five:

Naomi: Why won't Ruth go home? I gave her my blessing. I tried to set her free of any obligation that she feels towards me. I even told her that God has turned against me by taking my husband and sons away from me. But she won't listen. She insists she's coming with me and that nothing I can say will make her change her mind.

Narrator: Day six:

Ruth: I wonder what Naomi's village is like. Will her neighbours remember her? What will her relatives say when they find out about Elimelech and Mahlon and Chilion? What kind of reception will we get? Will they welcome Naomi, or will they resent her for leaving the village when they were all struggling for survival, for getting out with her husband and sons and leaving the weakest behind? And what will they make of me, with my foreign ways and accent? Will they blame me for what has happened? I'm not someone who was chosen by the God who they believe looks after them. Naomi thinks that her God is punishing her. Will he punish me too? I've said her God will be my God, but I don't know what he's like, this God of hers, or what he demands.

Narrator: Day eight:

Naomi: Ruth is still with me. Although her presence is a continual reminder of what I've lost, I'm not sorry. It's good to have a daughter-in-law who loves me like a daughter, like a friend. I'm trying to tell her about my village, my people, about our faith and traditions. But it's so strange to her. And how can I tell her that our God is generous and faithful, when all I feel is bitterness towards him because he has taken from me all that I lived for and love?

Narrator: Day nine:

Ruth: Naomi says we're getting near to Bethlehem. Part of me is excited and part of me is scared. This journey has given me time to think, time to ask questions. I don't feel like the person that I was when we left Moab. I've had to leave behind the things that I don't need any more, to let them go. And I've discovered some of the things that I want for myself, what I hope for, what I dream about, what I need. I can't forget Chilion, or Moab, or my family. I don't want to, they're still part of me, part of the story of who I am. And I know better who I am now. I am Ruth. I am a widow. I am strong. I am able to take risks and to make changes. I am travelling with a new God. Naomi says he looks after his people, fights for them, shelters them, feeds them. He sounds a bit more like a she to me. I'll tell Naomi that one day.

I wish I could share some of this with Naomi. She's so sad at the moment. I want her to know how much I love her, that I want to stay close to her, that I want us to share whatever happens to us from now on.

Narrator: Day ten:

Naomi: Home is a good place to be and today was both sad and wonderful: wonderful to see my friends and neighbours and catch up on ten years of news and gossip; sad to tell my story, to come home without my husband and sons. It's hard, and yet it feels somehow safe to be back with people who still believe that God loves them and cares for them. Maybe here I can learn to live with my sadness and pain.

This is my home and Ruth is the stranger here, but it's strange for me too. This place is both an ending and a new beginning for me, for both of us. Maybe out of our struggle and suffering something new will be born.

Narrator: And so Naomi returned from Moab, and Ruth the Moabitess, her daughter-in-law, came with her. And as they came to Bethlehem, the barley was ripening and it was harvest time.

Ruth Burgess

The wings of shelter (Ruth 1–4)

The Lord bless you for what you have done.
The Lord reward you for your faithfulness.
The Lord, the God of Israel under whose wings
you have come for shelter.

The Lord bless you, Ruth, for all that you have done,
for leaving home and family,
for leaving familiar land for an unknown country.
The Lord bless you for what you have done,
putting aside your own tears and your grief
to care for the widow Naomi.

The Lord bless you for what you have done.
The Lord reward you for your faithfulness.
The Lord, the God of Israel under whose wings
you have come for shelter.

The Lord bless you, Ruth, for all you have done,
for leaving all that was known and familiar
for an unknown country and a life of no status.

A widow in an alien land
with no prospects
but the grieving Naomi whose life indeed is bitter.

The Lord bless you for what you have done.
The Lord reward you for your faithfulness.
The Lord, the God of Israel under whose wings
you have come for shelter.

You have sown the seed of your deeds well, my daughter.
Now reap the harvest of your reward.

You have watered your deeds with the tears of your grief
and they have rooted in the barren soil of your mourning.

You have tilled the soil of kindness
and now your deeds are blooming
into blessing at the hands of Boaz.

The Lord bless you for what you have done.
The Lord reward you for your faithfulness.
The Lord, the God of Israel under whose wings
you have come for shelter.

The Lord has blessed you, Ruth.
Blessed you through the hands of Boaz.
No chance meeting in the cornfield
but a God-incidence, ordained indeed by God.

A godly man blessing all whom he meets,
an upright, wealthy man, and a relative.
A Kinsman-Redeemer who can bless you and save you
and extend care to Naomi too.

The Lord bless you for what you have done.
The Lord reward you for your faithfulness.
The Lord, the God of Israel under whose wings
you have come for shelter.

S Anne Lawson

1 Samuel

Don't worry, Hannah (I Samuel I, 2:1–21)

People used to say to me, 'Don't worry, Hannah, God will bless you in due course.' But they were just religious platitudes to me – spoken by those who were already mums! People who knew what it was like to be a real woman. They could not understand how childlessness diminished me. How it caused me sleepless nights. How it haunted me night and day. I longed – no ached – for the time I could be like them. I wanted to be able to play with my child, tuck them up in bed and tell them the stories my mother told me. I wanted to be able to laugh with them, and be there to wipe away their tears when they cried. I wanted all of that, but it was not to be. Years were passing by, and still no child to call my own. I even thought of suicide, for I felt so alone in the world, so forgotten, and Elkanah my husband did not understand.

So I prayed. Well, 'prayer' is maybe not the right word here. I made a bargain with God: Give me a child and I will give him back to be your servant! In the silence and emptiness of the sanctuary, I prayed with all my heart and mind and soul and tears poured down my face as I pleaded with God to bless me with a son. I got up to leave, when old Eli the priest came round the corner and said: 'May God hear your prayer.'

'Fat chance,' I said under my breath.

And then it happened. I was pregnant! Had God really answered my prayer? Was this some kind of miracle, or accident? I didn't care. I was overjoyed, overwhelmed – filled with hope beyond belief. But now I worried all through the pregnancy, fearing something might go wrong. Elated one moment, filled with fear the next. And if this child was truly of God, how was I going to keep my promise? How could I give up the child I had longed for? Had I bargained with God and lost? Or had I bargained with God and won? I did not fully understand this, and prayed harder and more frequently to find the strength to be what I had always wanted to be: a mother.

I named the child Samuel, because I had asked God for him, and that was what the name meant. So I had what I had longed for, a son, my only child! Yet, what about my promise to God that I would give him away in the service of the Lord? It would be an honour, a privilege to have a child in God's service, but after all the heartache, the pain and the desire, could I just give him away as promised? What mother could do that?, I reasoned with myself.

But I kept my promise. I asked Eli to take my child Samuel and train him in the ways of God. And I visited my son and clothed him year after year.

Julie Rennick, Spill the Beans

First encounters (1 Samuel 3:1–21)

An older Samuel looks back on his childhood encounter with God ...

The first time I ever heard God speak was when I was still young, living alongside my teacher Eli, who was so old and wise in my young eyes. I looked up to him in every way. My mother had told me to serve the Lord with all my heart and to learn from Eli what it meant to be a priest, a prophet, God's servant.

I had fallen asleep in my usual night-time corner of the temple, close to the ark of God's presence. Something woke me in the middle of the night, someone calling my name. I got up and ran to Eli, who came to at the sound of my footsteps and my asking, 'What is it? I'm here, sir!'

But whatever I'd heard, it wasn't Eli. It happened a second time, after I'd fallen asleep again – someone calling, 'Samuel! Samuel!' It made me nervous. If it wasn't Eli, then who was in the temple and what did they want? Where was the voice coming from and why was it calling out to me, a child, and not to my master the prophet? And why didn't Eli know who it was or why it was happening?

The third time it happened, Eli had begun to think harder. He told me to give the voice an answer: to tell it I was listening, to let it say what it wanted to say.

I had hardly pulled my blanket around me when the voice called for the fourth time. I sat up. 'Speak to me,' I said, and waited. 'I'm listening,' I said, not knowing what to expect.

Then I heard those terrible things, horrible stories, about Eli not stopping his sons from saying awful things against God, and how Eli would be punished. My wise, beloved old teacher was going to be punished, and no sacrifice or offering would change God's mind. No one had heard God's voice so clearly in years and years ... now here I was, just a boy, burdened with these terrible words, alone in the middle of the night.

I was terrified, lying there wide awake for hours in the darkness, clinging to my blanket trying not to cry. I wished I had never woken Eli. I wished he didn't know about the voice. But of course he asked me, 'What did the Lord say?'

I couldn't bear to answer, but he insisted that I be honest and spare him nothing. Did he somehow know or fear it was a word of judgement? Had he been carrying the shame of his sons' behaviour? Did he know that there would be a reckoning?

So I told him everything, fearing for what he might do when he heard it. But he did not tear his clothes or wail or cry. He did not beg for mercy or rush to make a sacrifice. He did not prostrate himself in prayer before the ark.

He was silent for a moment, then all he said was, 'It is the Lord. Let him do what seems good.' What seems good? I remember being astounded. Was this the God I had been told about but never encountered? A God who called on children to deliver messages of destruction to prophets who just accepted it as good if God said so? I wasn't sure I wanted to hear from this God again. However, as you know, the Lord had other ideas ...

Spill the Beans

Who knows best? (1 Samuel 3:1–21)

Who knows best – a grown-up or a child? Who is the wisest – someone very old or someone very young? Who would God speak to if God had something important to say – someone aged 60 or someone aged 6?

Grown-ups know more than children, right? Old people are wiser than young people, right? God would want to talk to a 60-year-old rather than a 6-year-old, right?

Here's a story to think about:

A long time ago, there was a very old man and a very young boy who worked together in God's temple. The old man, Eli, was a priest, and the little boy, Samuel, was learning how to be a priest. Now Eli had two sons who behaved very badly. Eli did nothing to stop them. God felt very unhappy about Eli's sons and when God saw that Eli did nothing to stop his sons from behaving so badly, God thought: I'm going to have to tell Eli how upset I am.

God wanted to be sure Eli got the message. Eli was an old man. Eli was a wise man. But God didn't go and talk to Eli. God decided to talk to the little boy Samuel who worked with Eli in the temple. Samuel had never heard God speaking before. But one night when Samuel was fast asleep in his bed, God gently called out his name and woke him up.

At first Samuel thought it was Eli shouting for him. Eli thought Samuel must have been dreaming. But God kept calling, 'Samuel! Samuel!' Until at last Eli said, 'It must be God who is calling your name!'

So Samuel listened to God and heard how upset God was about Eli's sons and their bad behaviour. Samuel was scared to tell Eli what God had said. It was a hard thing for Eli to hear. He had let God down by not telling his sons that they needed to behave with more respect and kindness.

So Eli the priest listened to the little boy Samuel, and Eli understood that God does not always speak to a grown-up when something important needs to be said. God does not always choose to talk to an old person or a wise person. Sometimes children can be the best listeners, the best hearers, even when it is a difficult message that God wants to pass on.

Spill the Beans

Music therapy (1 Samuel 16:14–23)

Sometimes I would get to the end of my tether.
Some days I would be at my wits' end.

The 'sometimes' and the 'some days' would get more frequent.
Myalgic encephalomyelitis was little understood back then
(but at least I'd learned to say the words and not just say M.E.).
Little understood by the medical profession.
Little understood by people.
Little understood by the press.
'Yuppie flu', they used to call it.
So, little understood by my colleagues
and least of all understood by us.
What we did understand was that my wife suffered from it.
What we did understand was how debilitating it is.
What we did understand was that we had two small boys who
also needed looking after.
What we did understand was that we were getting very little help.

Sometimes I would get to the end of my tether.
Some days I would be at my wits' end.

Looking after my wife and my ministry,
laundry and my ministry,
cooking and my ministry,
cleaning and my ministry,
getting the boys to school and my ministry.
Plus the Big Question: would she get better, and when?
It was all very worrying,
all very tiring,
all very stressful.

Sometimes I would get to the end of my tether.
Some days I would be at my wits' end.

At those times, on those days, I found myself picking up my guitar.
Always the same song:
Dylan's 'All along the watchtower'.
Why that particular song?
Maybe the words?
Maybe the riff?
Maybe both?
I don't know.
I do know I always felt much better afterwards.

Sometimes I would get to the end of my tether.
Some days I would be at my wits' end.

Then I'd sing 'All along the watchtower'.
Then go and cook the tea.

David Hamflett

Winner takes all (1 Samuel 17)

Do you enjoy a challenge?
Do you want to achieve fame?
Are you patriotic?
Do you have military or martial arts experience?
We are urgently seeking to appoint a national representative for this once-in-a-lifetime contest with the Philistines.
All armour and weapons provided.
Full medical assistance available if required.

Kathy Crawford

And what did Goliath do then, daddy?
(1 Samuel 17)

And what did Goliath do then, daddy?

Well, nothing, he just died.

When the stone hit him, did he scream and roll around in agony?

No, he just fell down.

When David cut his head off, did blood spurt all over the place?

There was some blood, yes.

Did everyone cheer when he died?

We, the Israelites, all cheered.

I bet all the good people in the whole world cheered, didn't they, daddy?

Possibly.

I bet Goliath's mum cheered, because I expect he was a really naughty boy who was rude to his parents and never did what he was told.

Well …

I bet Mrs Goliath and the children all cheered because he was cruel to them and they were glad he was dead.

Er …

I bet all the Philistines cheered.

No, actually they didn't.

Well, then they were stupid.

Brian Ford

Michal's story (1 Samuel 19:20–29 and 2 Samuel 6:16–23)

I loved you.

I always loved you, from that first time you went out against Goliath, so small and vulnerable.

When the whole nation thought you were a hero, cheered you on and celebrated your victories, you were my hero too.

Even though I knew my father would use my love, sending you out against the Philistines again in the hope you would be killed, I loved you, and celebrated your safe return.

I loved you, even though my father saw you as an enemy and a threat, hunting you down to kill you.

I risked my life to save yours, deceiving my own father so that you could get away – and then you went into hiding, leaving me behind to face his fury.

Through all those long years when you were on the run – when my father married me off to someone else, and I heard you had other wives and children – I clung to the last shreds of my love.

When you returned, I waited and waited until you sent for me; and then, hopeful that at last we would make a life and family together, I came to you, leaving my broken-hearted husband behind.

But you never said you loved me. To you I was just 'Saul's daughter', giving you a right to the title of king – just another pawn in your game to be reclaimed like a piece of lost property when it suited.

And when I saw you dancing, rejoicing in your success, your victory, something cracked in me. The bitterness and resentment of years of being used in your political game of thrones just welled up. I could no longer watch from the sidelines, confined to the house. 'What do you think you're doing,' I yelled, 'leaping about making a fool of yourself, half-naked in front of all the staff? Some king you are!'

That was it, of course. Oh, you said it was about worship of your God, but I'd pricked the bubble of your self-importance. I knew that was something you could not forgive. It was over between us from that moment. No love, no children, no future.

And yet – I loved you.

Jan Berry

2 Samuel

A joyful noise (2 Samuel 6:1–5)

Andy is banging a drum, or playing castanets – or just making a lot of noise!

Andy: Here we go, here we go, here we go!

Ada: Andy! What are you doing – and where are we going?

Andy: *(continues making lots of noise while dancing to music and singing to the tune 'Oh, when the saints go marching in')* Oh, when King David goes marching in, when King David goes marching in, oh, we're gonna be in that number, when King David goes marching in!

Ada: *(goes face to face with him)* Andy! Andy! Andy! Shut up!

Andy: *(taking earplugs out of his ears)* What are you saying, Ada?

Ada: I am telling you to shush up. What kind of racket is that to make in church?

Andy: I am singing a joyful song to the Lord.

Ada: Andy, I hate to tell you, we are Presbyterian. We don't do joyful!

Andy: How come?

Ada: Well … er … em … being joyful is a thing of the Devil!

Andy: Oh no it's not!

Ada: Well, I mean it can't be very biblical being joyful.

Andy: Are you kidding? 'Shout for joy to the Lord, all the earth. Worship the Lord with gladness; come before him with joyful songs' it says in Psalm 100.

Ada: Yes, well …

Andy: And what about this one from those priestly guys in the book of Deuteronomy who encouraged the people to: 'Be joyful at your festival – you, your sons and daughters, your male and female servants, and the Levites, the foreigners, the fatherless and the widows who live in your towns.' Chapter 16, verse 14. And there's lots more in the Bible about being joyful and happy.

Ada: Yes, okay, Andy, I get your point, but dancing. Surely dancing is not allowed in the church?

Andy: Why not? The psalmist told us: 'Praise his name with dancing and make music to him with tambourine and harp.'

Ada: Really?!

Andy: Yes, and Miriam danced with her sisters when Moses crossed the Red Sea!

Ada: But …

Andy: And remember that God 'turned my wailing into dancing; he removed my sackcloth and clothed me with joy'. Psalm 30:11.

Ada: However, Andy, that was a long time ago. We don't do that kind of thing now!

Andy: Why not? God wants us to be happy?

Ada: Yes …

Andy: And when I am happy I like to dance. *(Andy attempts a 'daddy' dance.)*

Ada: Yes, but …

Andy: And surely anything we do to praise God's holy name is good?

Ada: Yes … but …

Andy: Ada, there are no ifs, buts or maybes here. Our worship can be as noisy, as joyful and as bright as we want it to be. We can throw in a wee dance if we like, and we can clap along to the songs, and even shout Amen at the end of the sermon!

Ada: Oh no, I couldn't do that, Andy. My mother would turn in her grave!

Andy: Ada, we are not here in church to please our mothers or fathers, our granny or our grandpa. We are not here to please the minister, or to make us look good. We are here to praise God in every way we can.

Ada: Well, maybe I could give it a try just this once.

Andy & Ada: *(Andy hands Ada a percussion instrument and they begin to sing.)* Oh, when King David goes marching in, when King David goes marching in, oh, we're gonna be in that number, when King David goes marching in! …

John Murning, Spill the Beans

Building buildings (2 Samuel 7:1–17)

Andy: Hey, Ada, is this not a beautiful church building?

Ada: It certainly is, Andy.

Andy: I just love the stained-glass windows, the high ceilings …

Ada: And that lovely big pipe organ.

Andy: And that beautiful communion table that weighs about a ton, Ada.

Ada: So you tell me every time you try to lift it!

Andy: Well, Ada, it is really heavy, and so are those three big chairs. Solid, so they are!

Ada: Okay, Andy, I think we get that! However, I also like the baptismal font. Did you know it was gifted by my great auntie Nettie?

Andy: Aye, and did she not also gift some of the flower vases for the floral displays, Ada?

Ada: She did, Andy, very generous woman, my great auntie Nettie.

Andy: Didn't leave a bean to any of the family though. Left the rest of her money to the cat and dog home!

Ada: She was a bit eccentric right enough … but nice!

Andy: Eccentric does not begin to describe her!

Ada: *(gently changing the subject)* Anyway, Andy, why are you getting all sentimental about the church? The presbytery aren't going to close us down, are they?

Andy: Nothing like that, Ada. I just think it is a beautiful place, as though it was built for God himself!

Ada: Oh, I see where you are going with this.

Andy: You do?

Ada: Of course I do. Andy, I can read you like a book.

Andy: Eh, well, mmm! So what do you think I was going to say?

Ada: *(sounding pleased about her wisdom)* You were going to say something about the church as God's dwelling place, and how we have to look after it, and keep it beautiful.

Andy: Well, Ada, I was actually going to ask why we need a church at all.

Ada: Ah, so the presbytery *is* going to shut us down?

Andy: Not at all. It's just this Bible passage today about David wanting to build God a place to live. God has always been with his people, wherever they were in the world. He went before them, came behind them, and surrounded them on every side to protect them and be with them. He never needed a building, until King David came up with the bright idea.

Ada: It sounds as though David wanted to do something special for God.

Andy: Well, Ada, I am not so sure that was his intention. I think he maybe wanted to control God, and keep him in the one place, and limit the free movement of God and his people.

Ada: Wow, do you really think that is what King David was thinking? That he got carried away with himself, and thought God would be happy in a solid building rather than the tent he had been carried about in up till then.

Andy: I think so. Maybe that is why God said to Nathan the prophet that it would be better to provide a home for all of God's people, rather than a home to keep God in one place.

Ada: So do you think churches, even ones like ours, are about keeping God inside rather than outside the building?

Andy: Well, Ada, I don't think it is possible to limit God in any way. His presence is not confined to one place, because God is everywhere. He is at much at home in the community as he is in the church. He is at home in heaven and on earth. He is at home wherever God's people are, and he is there to meet the needs of his people, and not to worry about the decorations of buildings in his memory.

Ada: So are you saying we don't need a church to worship God?

Andy: That's right, Ada. We don't need a fixed building.

Ada: However, does the building not reflect to everyone else that God is in this place? It stands as a symbol of God's people for everyone to see.

Andy: Indeed, it does, Ada, but as long as the church itself does not try to take the place of God.

Ada: Heaven forbid it, Andy!

Andy: Heaven forbid it indeed, Ada!

John Murning, Spill the Beans

Rewriting the plans (2 Samuel 7:1–17)

Nathan approaches David to break the news that God is not enthused about the ideas discussed the previous day. Nathan begins hesitantly and nervously.

Nathan: *(feigning lightheartedness)* Good morning, your majesty.

David: *(upbeat and a bit distracted)* Morning, Nath!

Nathan: Good night's sleep, sir?

David: No! I was wide awake all night – it was wonderful! I've got so many ideas for the Lord's house!

Nathan: *(almost to himself)* I was afraid of that …

David: *(enthusiastically)* The best cedar, the finest gold …

Nathan: Erm … your majesty …

David: *(not really listening)* A grand porch and pillars …

Nathan: But sir, there's just one problem …

David: *(really looking at Nathan for first time)* Problem, Nath? Oh, look at you, didn't you get much sleep either?

Nathan: *(unhappily, hesitantly)* I was, em, dreaming.

David: Dreaming! Yes! Isn't it wonderful to dream! What did you dream for this house we're going to build?

Nathan: *(becoming bolder)* The Lord had something to say about that.

David: He did?! How amazing! Well, what does he want? Bronze? Copper? How many pillars? Did he say how big the whole thing should be?

Nathan: *(confidently now)* His message wasn't quite along those lines, your majesty.

David: Well, tell me then, Nath! What is the word from the Lord?

Nathan: (calm and matter of fact) He doesn't want a house.

David: (after a shocked silence) But … we have to! We need a place – for the Lord to dwell!

Nathan: He doesn't want a house. God has lived with us and moved with us ever since our ancestors left Egypt, and has never asked that we build him a house.

David: But look at this house of mine – my refuge and my haven! I can't give God any less!

Nathan: I think that may be precisely where he sees things differently.

David: Now you've lost me.

Nathan: To build the Lord a house would be to give him less. We cannot put the Lord in any building, your majesty. Cedar and stone can never contain his presence.

David: (pausing, and then arguing from another angle) But the people need a place to go, somewhere strong and solid and tangible, as a sure sign that God is with us.

Nathan: It would not take long for those static walls and fixed adornments to be seen as a 'sure sign' that God has settled down and is standing still.

David: (disappointed) But they would be so beautiful, the porch and the pillars …

Nathan: Pillars of fire and cloud; the beauty of mountains, valleys, stars: this is how we have known the Lord.

David: But it seems such a wonderful dream.

Nathan: The Lord's dreams are far bigger than ours. The promise is that God will build you a house!

David: (more excited, intrigued) Not of wood and ore?

Nathan: Of body and spirit, your majesty! A people in which the Lord will live! Learning, loving, growing, moving on together! And your name – David – they will always speak of as a testimony to where they come from and who they are.

David: (amazed and humbled) Bless the Lord! May he build the house he deserves, and may we live up to our place in it.

Jo Love, Spill the Beans

Bathsheba's dilemma (2 Samuel 11:1–15)

An emotion-charged dialogue between Bathsheba and the wife of Joab, Jemimah

Jemimah: Bathsheba! There you are.

Bathsheba: Jemimah! Thank God you're here.

Jemimah: I've just heard the terrible news.

Bathsheba: It can't be worse than what I need to tell you.

Jemimah: Bathsheba –

Bathsheba: (interrupting) Listen, this is more important. Have you heard from Joab? Do you know if the men are coming home soon?

Jemimah: (hesitant, bewildered) Coming home soon? You really haven't heard, have you?

Bathsheba: (urgently) Jem, I need to see Uriah! I mean, I need him to come home. I need him to … lie with me.

Jemimah: Lie with you? Don't you know what's happened?

Bathsheba: I know what's happened all right! I'm pregnant, Jem, and it isn't Uriah's baby.

Jemimah: What?! He goes off fighting and you're with another man?

Bathsheba: *(indignant)* No! Jem, I need to see my husband, to cover up what has been done to me.

Jemimah: *(dawning on her what Bathsheba is talking about)* Done to you? Then you should shame this man! Who is he? He should be stoned!

Bathsheba: No! If Uriah comes home soon, it will look like the child is his.

Jemimah: It's too late, Bathsheba.

Bathsheba: No, it's not too late, it's only been a month.

Jemimah: But … *(pausing)* … Uriah was sent home from duty one night last week. Joab was puzzled, because the king insisted on it.

Bathsheba: The king sent him home? So he thought of the same cover-up. But my husband didn't come to me. So it didn't work. Uriah is too honourable.

Jemimah: *(aghast)* You don't mean? … Tell me you're not saying …

Bathsheba: Yes. I am with the king's child. Don't you see I can do nothing against him?

Jemimah: Now it all makes sense. Oh no! ……

Bathsheba: What is it?

Jemimah: When Uriah returned, Joab received a second message from the king.

Bathsheba: What message?

Jemimah: To put Uriah on the frontline, in the heaviest fighting …

Bathsheba: No! Is he safe? Have you heard?

Jemimah: That's why I came to find you.

Bathsheba: *(trying not to hear the inevitable)* Why? ... Why did you come? ...

Jemimah: I just heard ... the terrible news ... It's too late, Bathsheba ... He has fallen. He is dead.

Bathsheba: *(utterly devastated)* Noooo! Uriah, Uriah ... O God, help me ...

Jo Love, Spill the Beans

A small lamb (2 Samuel 12:1–9)

A long time ago there was a king called David and a prophet called Nathan. One day Nathan said to King David: 'David, I have a story to tell you. Tell me what you think of it:

'There once was a rich person and a poor person living in the same town. The rich man was very rich. You could see that in the number of cattle and sheep he owned. The poor man was very poor, and you could see that in the number of sheep he owned: just one, a small lamb. The poor man loved his sheep and it lived with the family, was well looked after, and was even fed from the same bowls as the family and in the evening fell asleep in the poor man's arms. One day, the rich man received a guest and, as was the custom, he fed the traveller, showing him great hospitality. It was a huge meal he gave the traveller as he could well afford it, but instead of using one of his own lambs, the rich man stole the one from the poor man.'

Before Nathan could ask David how he felt about what happened in the story, David was burning with rage. He said, 'The rich man should be punished and should pay for that lamb four times over!'

There was a pause as Nathan looked at David, who looked back at Nathan wondering what the point of the story was. Nathan drew breath and said to King David, 'You are that man!' David remained silent but his anger was growing.

Nathan continued, 'The Lord says to you: "I have given you so much; I have saved you from your enemy; I have made you rich and powerful. I have made you King of Israel. So why do you hurt me by doing all the wrong you do? You killed Uriah the Hittite and took his wife. You are just like the rich man in Nathan's story who stole a poor man's lamb."'

And Nathan left King David to think about what he'd done.

Spill the Beans

Rizpah's sisters: mourning as resistance (2 Samuel 21:1–14)

Rizpah, the daughter of Aiah, used sackcloth to make a shelter for herself on the rock where the corpses were, and she stayed there from the beginning of harvest until the autumn rains came. During the day she kept the birds away from the bodies, and at night she would protect them from wild animals. (Sam 21:10, GNB)

Rizpah has become a model and inspiration for women all over the world. I have found references to her in Malaysia, Ghana, Latin America, South America, Germany, Russia …

In Argentina mothers and grandmothers of the Disappeared acted like her in their silent marches in the Plaza de Mayo, raising the questions: 'Where are our sons and daughters? What happened to our children and grandchildren who were stolen and placed in foster families?'

In apartheid South Africa students of theology worked on the resistance of Rizpah to find hope and strategies to overcome hopeless situations.

In Germany Rizpah is found in liturgies to overcome the desolate loss of fathers and sons in the Second World War. And through remembering all the lost ones, there came a forgiving and an understanding of the enemy: atonement and reconciliation.

In Russia mothers who helped their sons survive in the Russian military system are related to Rizpah without knowing her.

When I worked in Israel and Palestine as a human rights observer with the Ecumenical Accompaniment Programme of the World Council of Churches (EAPPI), Rizpah was my companion – at the huge Gilo checkpoint in Bethlehem, in desperate situations, and facing the humiliating behaviour of soldiers.

All the women and men demonstrating at Faslane nuclear base, praying and coming to witness and to protest again and again – are they not acting like Rizpah, are they not inspired by her? …

Rizpah's sisters, and some brothers, of our time are driven by the same divine spirit: to go out and name hopeless situations and act as agents of change and makers of peace.

Elisabeth Christa Miescher

I Kings

What should the king do? (1 Kings 12:1–29)

A long time ago there was a new king who needed some advice. He was called Rehoboam, but let's call him King Reb for short.

The people in his country were feeling pretty tired and upset. Their last king, who was called Solomon, had made everyone work far too hard. They had to survive on very little money because he took so much tax from them.

Everyone hoped that Reb would be much fairer than Solomon. Everyone hoped that Reb would be a kinder king and make life a bit easier, so they could work hard but not get so tired, and pay their taxes, but still have enough money to live on.

Reb decided to ask some friends for advice about how he should treat his people. How should he behave? Should he be kinder and fairer than Solomon, or should he be just the same, or maybe even tougher? He asked some old friends, and he asked some young friends.

Before we find out what his friends said, imagine Reb came to us for advice. Spend time discussing this using these starter questions:

What would you tell him to do?

Why should he be fairer?

Why should he be tougher?

What might make him decide one way or the other?

Well, Reb's older friends said, 'Reb! The best thing to do is be fair and kind to people. Then they will like having you as king and they will do what you want, because you are good to them.' But Reb's younger friends said, 'Reb! The best thing to do is to be even tougher than Solomon! Make them work harder and show them you are in charge – you are the king!'

Who do you think Reb listened to?

Well, Reb decided to listen to his younger friends, and he told everyone he was going to get tough and they were going to have to work twice as hard!

It was a very bad choice to make.

For the people in Reb's country, life was never the same again. They had hoped things were about to get better, but King Reb made things much worse.

Jo Love, Spill the Beans

The widow of Zarapeth (1 Kings 17)

I barely noticed him by the town gate, the strange man
in ragged clothes, with wild hair and even wilder eyes.
I was preoccupied with how my son and I would survive.
The drought had hit hard – no water for the crops and animals
and, coming so soon after my husband's death,
it had been a hard year for us anyway –
now starvation was staring us in the face.
I'd gone to fetch firewood to cook the last
of our flour and oil: one final meal for the pair of us.
What we'd do after that, God knows;
with everybody in the same situation we couldn't even beg.
We had no one to turn to.
And then he spoke: 'Please give me a drink.'
I didn't think twice as I turned to him with my water jar.
After all, the first rule of hospitality in desert lands
is to give water freely to those in need.
But then I was brought up short.
'Bring me some food, too,' he said, quoting the second rule:
sharing your bread with the stranger. This was too much to bear.
'I can't,' I told him angrily, embarrassed and ashamed at my frugality.
'It's the last I have … then my son and I will starve to death,'
I added for good measure.
'Don't worry,' he said. 'God will provide.
If you do this for me, there will be more than enough for all.'
And do you know, amazingly, there was.

Carol Dixon

Ravens above (1 Kings 17)

His God told him I could feed him. His God sent him to me. Me!
A woman with nothing.
A woman convinced her next meal would be her last.
A widowed woman expecting to die of starvation.
Of course, what a great choice his God made, picking me!
A hungry stranger sent to me. And he asked me for bread.
What was I supposed to do?
I had no bread.
And pitiful little flour and oil to make any more.
How terrible to have to tell a stranger that you can't feed them.
Never in my life have I had to turn round and say no.
Well, I didn't say no, exactly.
I couldn't bring myself to say it quite that bluntly.
After a lifetime priding myself on welcoming strangers
and feeding anyone who came to my door,
now my last act on earth was going to be
a refusal to look after this man.
Ah, you might say,
but what does hospitality matter when you're about to die?
That's the thing, it mattered a lot to me!
Was I about to die in shame as well as in hunger?

I told him I was going home to use
the last of my flour and oil for my son and myself.
I thought the man would understand.
I thought he might say some word
of release or blessing from his God,
that I would be forgiven for failing in my duty to him.
Instead he said I should bake for him first,
then for me and my son!
I laughed and I groaned, but it got worse.
He made wild claims that my oil and flour
would never run out until the rains came.
Was he already so hungry he was losing his mind, the poor soul?
I just nodded and went off home.

I was in a daze, going through the motions,
pouring the flour, pouring the oil, kneading the dough,
all the time watching my son, praying.
What would it matter to have endless bread,
what would it matter to see this stranger fed,
if I lost my boy?
I wondered if his God heard me, if his God was cruel.

But the wild claims about the oil and flour came true –
we had food enough – I don't know how.
I was astounded and grateful beyond words,
but just as all seemed well,
my boy began to slip away,
fevered and breathless.
Why? Why give me hope then take it away?
Why not let us die together in hunger but at least in peace?
Why send a stranger to my door who brings such trouble?

Yet he shared my agony, this man. He questioned his God.
The man cared about my son, not merely his own stomach.
He made no more wild claims of miraculous happenings,
he just stayed by my son and cried to his God.
I could not bear to be in the room.
When the crying stopped, it felt like my heart stopped.
I waited for him to come down
and tell me what I dreaded to hear.
But then I heard another cry.
Weak but familiar and calling for me. My dearest boy!
Was this man a prophet then?
A man of God, surely.
All he said was he had once been saved from starving
by wild birds, so it was not so hard to trust me.
Strange the things that give us faith.

Jo Love, Spill the Beans

Playing with fire (1 Kings 18:20–39)

A reflection through the eyes of a prophet of Baal. How might the 'losing side' have told the story?

There were 450 of us and one of him. And he decided to take us on. It all started with his shouting, goading us, accusing us of limping along unable to make up our minds about who is the most powerful in this land. He wanted to push us off the fence and choose: his God or our God, his truth or our truth? Contests like that have no winners. What was he trying to prove? How foolish we were to let him get under our skin with his irritating jeers.

My God is bigger than your God. So he wanted it settled? Whose God is better? Whose truth is right? Fine, let's settle it, a quick showdown should give him the showing up he deserves. He wanted fire, he wanted a freak show. How foolish we were to start dancing to his tune. He mocked us but we were making a mockery of ourselves. We were turning our own devotion into a crazed and desperate frenzy. Why would Baal deliver fire on cue for this foreign heckler? What was this game of gods supposed to achieve? Why were we competing for some hollow sense of supremacy?

There were 450 of us and yet, alone, his aggravating little presence had us hooked and sucked right in. And the longer it went on, the more humiliated we became, and our anger against him rose. What would it take to stop this absurd argument, to halt it in its tracks? Why did we not cease our hysteria, sit down and see the pointlessness of this power game? But he was pushing our buttons hard and we were driven to saving face.

Of course there was no fire. We were defeated but still that was not his moment of claiming victory. He carried on to an ever more bizarre spectacle, pouring water on the wood until it ran like a moat, and then screaming out with one long shout to whoever he believed was there. And with a sudden crack, the altar he had built caught fire! The heat of it scorched our faces and terrified our minds and we cried our allegiance in the face of the flames.

Then he believed he had won. Then he believed that settled it. He goaded us to a fight we didn't ask for and delivered a spectacle that brought no lasting change. What was he trying to do? And where did he go?

Jo Love, Spill the Beans

What are you doing here, Elijah? (1 Kings 19)

Where do you look for God?
Where does God find you?
Big questions!

Enter Elijah, the prophet of God.

Elijah was in trouble.
Jezebel the Queen wanted him dead.
Elijah ran.

First of all
he ran into the wilderness
and sat down under a broom tree,
the only tree for miles.

Elijah talked to God.
'God, I've had enough. I don't want to go on. Let me die.'

Silence.

Praying is hard work.
Elijah was tired.
He lay down under the broom tree and went to sleep.

Silence (well, maybe a few snores).

Someone shook Elijah.
'Get up, Elijah.
Have something to eat.'

Elijah could smell baking.
He opened his eyes.
There was a warm cake on the hot stones.
There was a big jar of water.

Someone was looking after him.
The cake was good.
The water was fresh.
Elijah ate and drank.

Eating and drinking is hard work.

Elijah lay down under the broom tree and went back to sleep.

Silence (well, maybe the odd sigh).

Someone shook Elijah again.

He could still smell baking.
'Eat up, Elijah,
you need strength for your journey.
It's time to go.'

Elijah woke up.
He ate more cake.
He had a long drink of water and he went.

Fast forward forty days and forty nights.

Elijah has travelled, further into the desert to Mount Horeb.

Travelling is hard work.
Elijah found a cave, lay down and went to sleep.

Silence (well, maybe the odd bat squeaking in the cave).

The next morning God arrived in Elijah's mind with a question.

'What are you doing here, Elijah?'

Silence.

Then Elijah answered.
He told God how tired he was.
He told God how scared he was.
He told God he wanted to die.

Silence.

And God said to Elijah,
'Go out to the cave mouth and watch.
I am coming to talk to you.'

Elijah stood and watched.

A great wind started up –
it was so strong that it was breaking pieces off the rocks.
Elijah struggled to keep standing.
God was not in the wind.

An earthquake rumbled and shook the ground under Elijah's feet.
God was not in the earthquake.

A fire blazed, crackling and spitting, flames dancing high and wild.
God was not in the fire.

And after the fire there was silence – sheer silence.
No groans, no snores, no sighs, no wind, no fire, no earthquake –
just silence.

In his mind, in his heart, in his body.
Elijah heard and felt the silence
and walked out of the cave into God's presence.

God spoke:

'What are you doing here, Elijah?'

And Elijah answered, and then he listened to God.

Where do we look for God?
Where does God find us?
Good questions to ask!

Ruth Burgess, Spill the Beans

Translators' paradox (1 Kings 19)

Is it merely interpretative choice:

the still small voice
or
the sound of sheer silence?

There's a loud difference between the two:
God's presence intimately perceived
or
God's absence tantalisingly vacant.

It speaks to us of:

God's immanence seen amid our experience
or
God's transcendence viewed from afar.

Perhaps we need both:

to do justice to the paradox of God,
to attempt to describe the indescribable.

Judith Jessop

The king and the queen and the vegetable patch (1 Kings 21)

Jezebel had grown up in a king's palace. Her father was the King of the Phoenicians. She was HRH Princess Jezebel. She was her father's and mother's daughter. She was well versed in the ways a princess should behave and had been well prepared for her future role as a powerful queen.

As often happens with princesses, Jezebel was given in marriage to a king of a neighbouring country for a political reason. In her case she was married to protect the important trade routes between two nations and to increase their military power.

The king Jezebel had been married to was called Ahab. He was the King of Israel.

Although their two nations were geographically very close to each other, they were very different places. They worshipped different gods, they had different value systems, and one nation lived by the sea, and the other nation lived in arid desert.

And as for Jezebel and Ahab, they were very different people.

Trouble lay ahead.

Our story begins in the royal palace …

Enter Queen Jezebel, who finds King Ahab curled up on his bed, facing the wall, crying and refusing to eat.

Jezebel enquires as to what is his problem.

'I wanted a new vegetable patch,' said Ahab sadly.

'Vegetable patch? You're crying about a vegetable patch?!' said Jezebel.

Ahab rolled up into a ball and began to sob.

'Ahab,' said Jezebel, 'stop behaving like a baby and tell me what all this is about!'

So Ahab told her.

He had been that morning to talk to a man called Naboth, who lived next door to the palace. Ahab had asked Naboth if he could buy his vineyard, as he wanted to create a new vegetable garden near to the palace – and Naboth had refused to sell it to him.

Jezebel was stunned.

'Is that all?' she said. 'Is that why you are crying and refusing to eat?'

Ahab sniffed and nodded.

Jezebel was appalled. This was no way for Ahab to behave. If he was not careful his people would walk all over him … and her.

'You're a king,' she told Ahab. 'You need to start behaving like one! Now get up and eat and look cheerful. I'll sort out this Naboth for you. His vineyard will soon be yours.'

Ahab didn't know what to do. No woman had ever spoken to him like that before! In his country, women were told what to do by their husbands.

However, having heard her, Ahab thought he'd better let Jezebel have her way.

Jezebel soon got to work. She knew that the nation's elders and nobles wouldn't listen to her. Unlike in her own country, the men of Israel didn't share their power with women. So she forged Ahab's name, and borrowed Ahab's royal seal and used it to seal all her letters.

Her letters brought all the elders and nobles together, and she bribed two trouble-makers to tell lies about Naboth, and in one short afternoon she managed to get Naboth accused, found guilty, sentenced to death, taken outside the city walls and killed.

Now that, thought Jezebel, is the way that things ought to happen round here!

And Jezebel dismissed the elders and nobles and went to find Ahab.

'Get your servants into their gardening gear,' she told Ahab. 'The vineyard is yours. Naboth is dead.'

Ahab was astounded, and a bit ashamed, but he'd got what he wanted – a vegetable patch close to home. And a very efficient wife as well!

The next day Ahab set off to inspect his new plot, and there was someone waiting there to see him. It was Elijah, God's prophet.

Elijah didn't waste words.

He told Ahab that God said that allowing evil to happen was the same as doing evil yourself.

And he told Ahab that he was as responsible as Jezebel for taking Naboth's life.

'Watch out,' said Elijah. 'For you and for Jezebel, disaster is coming.'

And Elijah went away.

You know Elijah and Jezebel never met.

Ahab was always the go-between.

And in some ways Elijah and Jezebel were quite similar.

Both powerful.

Both true to what they believed in.

Both loyal to those they loved.

So was Jezebel pure evil?

The writer of this book of the Bible would have us believe so, but me, I'm not so sure …

Ruth Burgess, Spill the Beans

I am Jezebel (1 Kings 18–21)

I am Jezebel, my very name a byword for immorality.

I was a Phoenician princess. Probably as part of some strategic military or trading alliance, I was packaged up and sent off to marry King Ahab of Israel. I was about 14 at the time. I didn't know anybody in Israel. I didn't speak the language and as a follower of Baal had a different religion.

I don't think it's fair how the men in this story get off the hook, and all the blame is placed on me. Elijah killed all Baal's prophets by putting them to the sword: religious genocide. And Ahab was the king. He was supposed to be in charge. He uses that age-old excuse, 'She told me to.' So, why am I the bad one?

There is another thing I want to set straight. I am not a prostitute or a promiscuous woman. Their only evidence for that claim is that I wore make-up!

Try to read between the lines. Remember the young girl with no choices forced into marriage in a strange land. Consider whose point of view the writer is taking. I was not blameless, but neither were they. There are two sides to every story.

Liz Delafield

Growing cucumbers (1 Kings 21)

King Ahab lived in Samaria in a royal palace. King Ahab liked growing things. The palace gardens were full of fruits and vegetables. There were beans and apples and grapes and dates and figs and melons and leeks and olives and lentils and pomegranates and onions and pistachio nuts. The problem was that the garden was so full of fruits and vegetables that there was no room to plant anything else, and King Ahab fancied having a go at growing cucumbers. What could he do? There was nothing for it. He needed a bigger garden.

Next door to the palace lived a man called Naboth. Naboth liked growing grapes and making wine and Naboth had a big vineyard. Ahab asked Naboth if he would sell him his vineyard. Naboth, whose family had owned the vineyard for years, said no.

King Ahab went home. He was cross, and then he was sad, and then he curled up on his bed and cried.

That night Queen Jezebel, Ahab's wife, waited for Ahab to come down to dinner and he didn't come. Jezebel was hungry so she ate her dinner and then went to find Ahab.

She found him in his bedroom and asked him what was going on. Ahab told her all about wanting a new vegetable garden in which to plant his cucumbers and about Naboth telling him he would not sell his land.

Jezebel was not impressed. 'You're a king,' she told Ahab. 'You can have whatever you want. Now stop crying and go and eat your dinner and leave Naboth to me.'

The next day Jezebel found some men who she paid to tell lies about Naboth. Then she forged Ahab's signature on some royal documents and had Naboth killed and his lands given to the king.

That night Jezebel told Ahab what she'd done.

Ahab was shocked. He knew what Jezebel had done was wrong. But he had got his new garden and that was what he really wanted. Did it matter how he'd got it?

The next morning Ahab went next door into Naboth's vineyard. He walked along the paths between the grapevines and began to plan where he was going to plant his cucumbers. He turned a corner and he met Elijah the prophet.

Elijah was not interested in cucumbers. He was there to tell King Ahab that God said that hurting people to get what you want was wrong.

And King Ahab knew that Elijah was right.

Ruth Burgess, Spill the Beans

2 Kings

Chariots of fire (2 Kings 2)

Have you ever had to take on someone else's job and not been sure if you could do it?

Listen to a story about Elijah and Elisha …

Elijah the prophet was going home to God. He was an old man now, and he was tired. Elisha the prophet had known for a long while that he was going to be the one who took Elijah's place. Elisha was scared.

How could he take over from Elijah? Elijah was famous; everyone knew about him. Elijah had challenged kings and queens, he'd lived with death threats, he'd performed miracles. It was even said that Elijah had been fed by an angel in the desert and that he'd seen God.

Elisha had a feeling in his bones that Elijah would be going soon.

Elisha went to find Elijah and they went on a journey together to a place called Bethel. Bethel means 'House of God' and it was quite a famous place. It was there, long ago, that a man called Jacob had dreamed about a stairway that climbed all the way to heaven.

Some wise men from Bethel came to speak with Elijah and Elisha. They too had a feeling that Elijah would be going soon. Elijah asked Elisha to stay in Bethel, but Elisha was determined to follow Elijah and see what happened. Just how was God going to take Elijah home?

So Elisha and Elijah travelled on to Jericho. Jericho was a beautiful city. It was known as the city of the palm trees. Travellers were always glad to reach Jericho.

Some wise men from Jericho came to talk with Elijah and Elisha. Again Elijah tried to persuade Elisha to stay behind but Elisha would not leave Elijah.

Elijah and Elisha travelled on from Jericho until they reached the banks of the River Jordan.

More and more people had heard about their journey and were curious about what was going to happen.

A group of men had been quietly following Elijah and Elisha. When they saw that Elijah and Elisha had stopped by the river, they stopped too and watched from a distance to see what would happen next.

Elijah took off his cloak and carefully rolled it up. Then Elijah struck the water with the cloak and the water rolled back. Some water went to the left and some to the right and a path appeared. Elijah walked across the path and Elisha hurried after him. They crossed the river without even getting their feet wet.

'Wow!' said one of the men watching. 'It's like Moses and the Red Sea all over again.' And then the water rolled back.

'Well,' said Elijah to Elisha, 'you know I'm going soon. I have a feeling you want something from me.'

Elisha nodded. They had a long talk. Elisha told Elijah he was scared about taking Elijah's job. And Elijah told Elisha about how he'd been scared too – especially when Queen Jezebel had threatened to kill him.

'But she didn't kill me,' said Elijah. 'And God looked after me. Whatever God asked me to do he was always there to help me do it. You'll be all right, Elisha. God will help you too.'

Elisha looked at Elijah. He said, 'I've known for a long time that I was to take your place. It's not going to be easy for me. Can you give me a double share of your power so that I can do my job well?'

'Watch!' said Elijah. 'If you see me go home to God, a double share of my power will be yours.'

By now they had walked out of sight of the men who were watching on the other side of the river and only Elisha saw what happened next.

The birds stopped singing and it was very quiet. Out of the sky came a huge chariot of fire and it was drawn by fiery horses. The chariot swooped down between Elisha and Elijah – it was all wind and flames and flashing hooves and swirling dust – and Elijah was taken from earth, right up to heaven, home to God.

Elisha had seen it happen. A double portion of Elijah's power was now his. Elisha tore his clothes as a sign that Elijah had gone home to God.

Elijah had left his cloak behind and Elisha picked it up. He walked back towards the river. The men on the other bank saw him coming. They saw that he was alone. They saw the tears in his clothes. And they saw that he was carrying Elijah's cloak.

'Where is the God of Elijah?' shouted Elisha.

It was a question for himself and it was a question for the men who were watching as well.

Elisha struck the River Jordan with Elijah's cloak and the river parted. Elisha walked across.

'Wow!' said one of the men who was watching. 'Elisha can do what Elijah could do!'

Elisha knew that God was with him and Elijah's power was in him.

He had a new job to do.

Ruth Burgess, Spill the Beans

Naaman and the dirty river of Jordan (2 Kings 5)

This needs nine readers: you need a narrator (longest part), Naaman, Naaman's wife, a young girl, King of Syria, King of Israel, Elisha, a messenger and a servant. Try to vary the ages of the readers.

Narrator: This is a story of an army commander and his wife, two kings, a young girl, a prophet, a messenger and some wise servants.

Naaman: I am Naaman. I am a commander of the army of the King of Syria. I have conducted many successful raids into surrounding countries, including Israel. I have brought back to my country prisoners and silver and gold.

Naaman's wife:	I am the wife of Naaman. I love him deeply. He is a brave and courageous man. One thing that he has not told you is that he is in the early stages of leprosy. As his leprosy grows worse, and it will, he will have to give up his job, and go and live in the wilderness, so that he does not give his leprosy to anyone else.
A young girl:	I don't have a name in this story. I was born in Israel. When I was a young child, Naaman's army took me prisoner and brought me to Syria. I have grown up in Naaman's household. I am a maid to his wife. I don't remember a lot about my early childhood but I do remember my parents talking about a man called Elisha. He was a holy prophet. He talked to people about God and sometimes sick people asked for his prayers and they were healed. I know how sad my mistress is about Naaman's leprosy. I told her about Elisha. He could cure Naaman.
Narrator:	So Naaman's maid talked to Naaman's wife and Naaman's wife talked to Naaman and Naaman decided to go and talk to the king.
The King of Syria:	I am the King Of Syria. Naaman has told me that he has heard about a man who lives in Israel who could cure his leprosy. That would be a wonderful thing to happen. I have written a letter to the King of Israel and given it to Naaman to take to him. I have also sent some silver and gold and some new clothes to put the King of Israel in a good mood.
Narrator:	So Naaman went to Israel. He took with him his servants, his horses and his chariots and the gold and the silver and the new clothes and the letter for the king.
The King of Israel:	I am the King of Israel. I don't know what to do. Naaman the commander of the King of Syria's army has just arrived at my court with all his chariots and horses and servants

and gold and silver and ten sets of new clothes and a letter from the King of Syria.

This is what the letter says. 'When this letter reaches you, know that I have sent you my servant Naaman, that you may cure him of his leprosy.'

I'm the King of Israel. I'm not God! I don't decide who lives and who dies. What can I do about Naaman's leprosy? The King of Syria is trying to pick a quarrel with me. I suspect that this is a new plot against Israel!

Narrator: The King of Israel was so upset that he tore his clothes. A sign of his despair.

Meanwhile in Israel news of Naaman's arrival had travelled fast. The people feared that Naaman might be spying out the land for another raid. And word came to Elisha about what was going on.

Elisha: I am Elisha. I am God's prophet in Israel. I tell and show people that God is strong and active. The King of Israel knows this. I want Naaman and the King of Syria to know this too.

Narrator: So Elisha sent a message to the King of Israel, telling him that there was no need for him to rip his clothes. And Elisha told the King of Israel to send Naaman to his house.

Naaman and all his servants and his horses and his chariots and the silver and the gold and the new clothes arrived at Elisha's house and stood outside the door. And Elisha sent out a messenger with a message for Naaman.

Messenger: I am the messenger, the servant of Elisha. This is what Elisha told me to say to Naaman: 'Go and wash in the River Jordan. Go and wash yourself seven times and your leprosy will be cured.' Naaman looked angry and he walked away.

Naaman: Of course I am angry. He didn't even come out to see me. I thought he would ask his God to heal me. I thought he would

	wave his hand over the sores on my body and cure my leprosy. Why should I wash in the River Jordan? It's a filthy river. The rivers in my land are better than all the rivers in Israel. I could wash in them and be clean! I'm not staying here to be insulted! I'm going home!
Narrator:	Naaman's servants had watched what was going on and one of them tried to talk to Naaman.
Servant:	I'm one of Naaman's servants. We can all see how upset he is. We don't know if this man Elisha can help Naaman, but we've come all this way, and we think that there's nothing to lose by doing what Elisha suggests. It might work.
	I took a deep breath and I asked Naaman, if the prophet had asked him to do a hard thing, would he have done it. Naaman said yes. So I took another deep breath and asked Naaman if he would do the easy thing that Elisha had asked.
	Naaman looked at me hard and long. He didn't say a word. Then he stripped off some of his outer clothes and handed them to me and waded into the River Jordan.
Narrator:	You can probably guess what happened next. Naaman ducked himself under the water one, two, three, four, five, six, seven times and when he came up the seventh time – his leprosy was gone. His sores had disappeared. His skin was like that of a young child.
	So that's the story of Naaman the army commander and his wife, two kings, a young girl, a prophet, a messenger and some wise servants. And as for the silver and the gold and the ten sets of new clothes, if you want to know what happened to them you can go home and read the rest of the story for yourselves.

Ruth Burgess, Spill the Beans

Advice from a batman (2 Kings 5)

A quiet word in your shell-like,
if I may ... er,
sir.
Now that matters have calmed
since your altercation with the prophet this afternoon:
he of the bushy beard and shiny head,
looking as if his face is upside down.
Yes, that was a very bad joke.
And yes, that means I'm after something;
how well you know me, sir.
And yes, I have made your favourite lamb stew.

The lads have suggested that I have a word with you.
You could call this impudence or insubordination
and have me flogged,
or worse.
But I hope you won't.
Remember who nursed you through that fever at Kadesh?
Who tended that infected wound after the Battle of Madon?
And no one else can get your shaving water at just the right temperature,
not to mention the lamb stew.

Now I know it would be a bit of a humiliation to go back
and do what the old boy said
but I'm told that his god is quite big on humility.
And yes, it is a muddy little stream.
Our rivers are much more impressive.
But if he'd asked you to do something challenging
you'd have done it,
wouldn't you?

So why not do something easy.
Actually, I suspect that may be the point,
it's sort of symbolic,
demonstrating faith and trust.
I think the god is pretty keen on those too.
It will show you haven't earned your healing:
it's a gift from Old Baldy's god.
So why not give it a go?
You've nothing to lose but your leprosy,
sir.

Brian Ford

1 Chronicles

God's glory (1 Chronicles 16)

God was there before the worlds began.
His hand set stars in space,
spun worlds on their axes,
separated sea and sky and earth.
God made the wonders of the world
and set us in the middle of them.
And this making –
this making of all we see and know –
of star-filled oceans of space,
of seas bright and splashing,
of land covered with mountains, valleys,
cataracts and streams, astonishing creatures,
trees and flowers, tall and small,
blossoming, springing, singing, shining,
rustling, shouting, sighing, whispering,
furry, feathered, sleek, smooth,
cool, crisp, warm, soft
beautiful things –
this making reflects a fragment
(a hair's breadth, the width of a fingernail, the tip of a top of a point)
of the nature of God.

In God's word we learn
that the world reveals God's glory
and so do we.

Sometimes God shows power, sometimes gentleness.
Sometimes God seems huge and we seem very small.

But this we know:
God will always be here.
God will never give up on us.
God will never leave us.

God, who is more glorious than all the glories he has made,
more bright than any sun or star,
made us

and knows us
and loves us.

Praise God!

Julie Sharp

The substance of what belonged to King David (1 Chronicles 27:25–31)

These were the administrators of the substance of what was King David's:

Over the king's treasures in the royal storehouses: Azmaveth son of Adiel.

Over the local storehouses and the barns in the fields and villages and in the cities and watchtowers: Jonathan son of Uzziah.

Over those who till the ground: Ezri son of Chelub.

Over those who manage and work in the vineyards: Shimei from Ramah.

Over the wine vats and wine cellars: Zabdi from Shepham, father unknown.

Over the olives and sycamore-fig-trees in the Western foothills: Baal Hanan.

Over the stores of olive oil: Joash, father and birthplace unknown.

Over the herds of cattle in the plains of Sharon: Shirtai from Sharon.

Over the herds of cattle in the valleys: Shaphat son of Adlai.

Over the camels: Obil the Ishmaelite.

Over the donkeys: Jehdeiah from Meronoth.

And over the sheep and the goats: Jaziz who was a Hagrite.

These were the administrators of the substance of what was King David's.

King David was a very substantial man.

Ruth Burgess

David's prayer (I Chronicles 29:10-20)

God of Jacob, we bless you.
You are magnificent and full of glory.
You are able to make us strong.

The earth and the heavens belong to you.
Everything we have is a gift from you.
Everything we give you is already yours.

Our days are like a passing shadow.
We are here only for a short time.
None of us can run away from death.

You look into our hearts.
You are pleased when we are honest.
You look for integrity in our lives.

God of our ancestors, keep us faithful,
dance in our dreams, accept our offerings,
keep us always in love with you.

Help my son Solomon to build your temple.
Your temple, for which I have made preparations.
Give him a longing to walk with you.

Ruth Burgess

2 Chronicles

Solomon's wisdom (2 Chronicles 9)

Well, that was something.
The Queen of Sheba, no less, visiting me.
Gifts, jewels, gold, spices, quite a spread
from a visiting head of state.

She loved the splendour of the Temple,
she enjoyed the food,
but most of all she just wanted to be with me.

She had questions, lots of questions,
and I bantered back and forth with her,
answering as best I could.

'So wise,' she muttered as I spoke.
She even told my officials how privileged they were
to hear my wise pronouncements day by day.

Of course I played along,
who wouldn't?

But do I really feel this wise?

I'm worried that if I keep hearing people talk this way
I might begin to believe
that there is something special about me,
that I can do things no one else can do.

It doesn't feel that way.
When someone comes to me with their problem,
I just try to do the right thing,
try to make the sensible choice,
the choice that will reveal the truth,
if I can.

It doesn't feel very special.
In fact, most of the time it feels like compromise:
like trying to find an alternative way
to look at what one person says
against what the other person says.
I'm not picking sides,
just trying to find out what is true
and to help people work towards that.

Of course, the story has spread far and wide
of my request for wisdom from God
in knowing how to lead his people.
Perhaps it was granted to me,
but it seems to me it is not just knowledge,
the wisdom comes in reading people,
in knowing what is in their hearts.

Which is why I was more than happy
to send the Queen of Sheba back home
with more gifts than she arrived with,
for I am pretty sure I know what would have happened
if she had remained longer.

I have enough to worry about as it is.

Peter Johnston

The Queen of Sheba (2 Chronicles 9)

Here I am – a queen.

I am wealthy and powerful.

I have intellect.

I ask questions.

I am curious about this Lord God of Israel.

I am going to visit King Solomon.

It takes a lot to impress me but this is impressive – this is overwhelming.

I have brought with me a precious cargo of gifts, but they seem paltry compared with Solomon's possessions.

Even more impressive is how clearly he answers my questions. Whatever I ask, he responds wisely.

I recognise that the Lord God of Israel is pleased with him, with his justice and wisdom.

Travelling home, I marvel at what I have seen and at all Solomon has achieved. It seems as if the whole world respects him and listens to him.

And I have learnt that the Lord God of Israel expects King Solomon to obey Him and worship Him alone.

Now, back in my own kingdom, I am observing from afar Solomon's decline – the decline of a great and mighty king who has turned away from an even greater King.

How the mighty have fallen.

A lesson for this queen.

Pam Hathorn

Ezra

I remember it all (Ezra 1–4)

I'm old now,
but once I was young.
I remember it all:
the first temple in Jerusalem,
the long journey to Babylon,
the exile,
the longing for home,
and then God speaking through the words and actions of Cyrus,
the King of Babylon,
telling us that we could go home
and rebuild the temple –
God's house.

I remember the generosity of our neighbours in Babylon.
They gave us so much:
food for the journey,
animals,
silver pots and pans,
gold,
and Cyrus gave us back
all the gold and silver bowls and ornaments
that had been used in the temple –
all 5,400 of them.
This was never going to be a journey
where we travelled lightly!

Not everyone returned to Jerusalem and Judah
but many families did.
They reckon over 40,000 of us
came home to our villages and cities,
and someone said
we brought back 6,720 donkeys and 435 camels with us
and 736 horses and 245 mules.

It took us a few months to settle back into our old homes.
Many things had changed

and we'd changed too.
It wasn't easy.

But at last we were ready
to go to Jerusalem
and rebuild God's house,
God's temple.

As many as could,
old and young,
gathered in Jerusalem.

The priests offered sacrifices
on an altar
keeping the rules and customs
that had been laid down by Moses.

We celebrated the Feast of Shelters
remembering God's care for us
and hoping for good harvests to come
in our own lands.

Cedar trees were brought by sea from Lebanon
and the stone masons and the carpenters
made ready to begin.

And at last
the day came
to lay the foundations of the new temple.
What a day!
I can close my eyes and see it all so clearly.

The priests were there
dressed in their robes
and they blew trumpets
and the Levites
clashed cymbals,
the noise was deafening,
and everybody sang,

old voices and young voices,
babies crying,
donkeys braying.
We sang the words of King David
over and over again:

God is good.
God's love for Israel goes on for ever and ever.

God is good.
God's love for Israel goes on for ever and ever.

God is good.
God's love for Israel goes on for ever and ever.

We watched the foundations of the Temple being laid
and some people cried,
cried for all that had been lost,
all that had gone,
and others shouted for joy
that God had not forgotten his people,
that God was doing something new.

Shouts and tears,
laughter and mourning,
sorrow and joy
all mixed up together
in a noise so loud that you could hear it
far away.

I remember it all:
the smells, the sounds, the colours,
a mixture of the old customs
and new beginnings
and God's love in both.

I'm old now
but even for me
this is a time of opportunity,

a time of hope and change,
a time to build,
a time to love,
and a time to know that God is near
always
for ever and ever and ever.

Ruth Burgess, Spill the Beans

The foundation stone (Ezra 1–4)

Rachel was standing with her mum and dad in the crowd, and all sorts of things were going on.

There were lots of workers: the men who had chiselled the stone into the right shape, and the people who would move the stone into the right place to start making the building. The stone was huge. Rachel's father had told her that the first stone that was put into a building had a special name. It was called the foundation stone.

Rachel could see lots of her friends, who were there with their parents. It was a special day – and everyone was excited. Today, in Jerusalem, was the day that the foundation stone of the temple would be put into place.

They had been living in their village for seven months now and it was very different to Babylon where they had lived before. There were older people in the crowd; they could remember living in the village many years ago – for them they had come home – they had lots of memories – but for Rachel and her friends everything was new.

Suddenly there was a loud noise. Rachel's father lifted her onto his shoulders so that she could see what was happening. The noise was the sound of trumpets being blown, and then some people began to play the cymbals. And then people began to sing. They sang the same song over and over, and as Rachel listened and learnt the words she joined in too. Some people sang one line, and their friends sang another line back to them:

God is good.
Yes, God is good.

God loves us.
Yes, God loves us.

God loves us today.
Yes, God loves us today.

God loves us for ever.
Yes, God loves us for ever and ever and ever …

Slowly, and with lots of people pushing and pulling, the foundation stone was moved into its place and the people went on singing. Everybody sang – the old people, the workers, the mums and dads, the children and even the babies and the horses and donkeys joined in.

God is good.
Yes, God is good.

God loves us.
Yes, God loves us.

God loves us today.
Yes, God loves us today.

God loves us for ever.
Yes, God loves us for ever and ever and ever.

Rachel smiled; up on her dad's shoulders, she could see everyone. Some people were shouting because they were so happy. And Rachel noticed that some of the older people were crying. Rachel remembered that earlier in the day one old woman from their village had told her that she could remember the building of the first temple and that some of the things that she remembered were sad and some happy. As Rachel listened, the noise of the crying and the happy shouts and the song and the music all got mixed up together into a loud loud noise.

This was a day that Rachel would remember – the excitement, the music, the singing and the putting in place of the huge foundation stone of the Temple.

And when she grew up, this was a song that she would teach her children and her children's children:

God is good.
Yes, God is good.

God loves us.
Yes, God loves us.

God loves us today.
Yes, God loves us today.

God loves us for ever.
Yes, God loves us for ever and ever and ever.

Note: *If your building has a foundation stone you might like to go and look at it.*

Ruth Burgess, Spill the Beans

Yes, governor (Ezra 3–6)

On the rebuilding of Jerusalem, as seen by those who opposed it.

Cast (all officials of the Persian province of Trans-Euphrates, which includes Jerusalem):

Tattenai – Governor (posh but rather dim and concerned about his own reputation)

Rehum – High Commissioner (experienced with the levers of power)

Shimshai – Secretary to the Governor (well meaning but naive)

Mithredath – Councillor (schemer)

Setting: office (indicated by tables and chairs) of the Governor of Trans-Euphrates, approximately 500 BC. Actors may carry files or clipboards to hide their script. Cards or projected slides give the scene and time changes.

Scene 1:

Rehum: Well, Shimshai, how are you enjoying your post as secretary to Lord Tattenai, our new governor in Trans-Euphrates?

Shimshai: Ah, Commissioner Rehum, how kind of you to enquire. The governor is settling in well – seems to be taking quite an interest in local affairs.

Rehum: You will have to watch that, Shimshai. If Lord Tattenai gets to understand how we are running things here in Trans-Euphrates, there's a risk that our new king, Artaxerxes, might take an interest too. We wouldn't want that, would we?

Shimshai: Er, no, I suppose not. The last king, Cyrus, didn't take much notice of us, did he? – we are rather on the edge of the Persian empire.

Mithredath: The main thing he did for us was to invite all those Jews to settle in the ruins of Jerusalem – along with a massive grant from the Treasury.

Shimshai: I'd forgotten that – quite a fuss at the time, wasn't there? Shouldn't they have opened this new temple they're building by now.

Rehum: Perhaps – but they have been having a few problems.

Mithredath: Unfortunately the planning application got lost.

Rehum: And their drainage system was condemned by the sanitary inspector.

Mithredath: They were fined for a spelling mistake on their tax return.

Rehum: And some of their best workers found their work permits out of order.

Shimshai: But I thought we prided ourselves on having a very efficient administration here in Trans-Euphrates?

Mithredath: We do – when we want to.

Scene 2: 1 month later

Mithredath: Congratulations, governor, your insight into the needs of this province is impressive.

Tattenai: Thank you, Mithredath. One tries to help.

Mithredath: So, I feel I can share with you a concern we have had for some time: Jerusalem.

Tattenai: Jerusalem – ah, yes – disadvantaged minority faith, regeneration projects, all that sort of thing.

Mithredath: Well, it might seem that way, governor, but look at it from the point of view of the ordinary people of Samaria. They haven't had any imperial funds to build a temple. These Jews don't make any effort to assimilate you know. And they're not just building a temple – it's a walled city – to be used as a fortress.

Tattenai: You mean that if they finished the walls they could close the gates and keep us all out? *(Mithredath nods.)* Even the tax collectors? *(Mithredath nods.)* What can I do?

Mithredath: The Council feels that it would be better if the rebuilding in Jerusalem were to stop. It could become a centre of sedition – undermine the whole empire. In fact, it might be our duty to warn the king of the risks.

Tattenai: Yes – I do see your point. Don't want these chaps to get above themselves. And it doesn't hurt to let Artaxerxes know we're looking out for his interests.

Mithredath: So if you would just sign this letter to the king – we can get him to cancel the permission Cyrus gave them.

Tattenai: *(signing)* I imagine the idea of cancelling something Cyrus started might appeal to him.

Mithredath: Yes, governor.

Scene 3: 3 months later

Shimshai: The king has replied to the governor's letter about Jerusalem.

Rehum: And ...

Shimshai: It seems that when Artaxerxes got the letter he asked the Palace Research Department to look at the historical record on Jerusalem – and found it very worrying. Of course it used to be the centre of a kingdom and raise its own taxes – quite a troublesome city – rebellion against the monarchy and so on.

Rehum: Very sound research – and I'm sure the selected local recollections you sent in will have helped.

Shimshai: So the king wants us *(reading)* 'to issue orders that these men must desist. The city is not to be rebuilt ... See that you do not neglect your duty in this matter.'

Rehum: Oh, I'm sure we won't neglect that. Arrange a briefing for the governor and the commander of the army this afternoon.

Shimshai: Will there be fighting?

Rehum: We'll take soldiers when we deliver the order. But I doubt if there will be resistance.

Shimshai: Why not?

Rehum: Think about it, Shimshai. You've got a family. Imagine you'd come down to Jerusalem – a city of rubble. Once the first excitement has worn off, what would you rather be building – the walls? The temple? Or your own house?

Shimshai: I see ... So though they won't like being ordered about, they may not be sorry to stop building the walls and the temple?

Rehum: Precisely.

Scene 4: 10 years later

Tattenai: Next item – Jerusalem. I thought it had been quiet there for years?

Rehum: It had – but they seem to be taking advantage of the fact that we now have a new king, Darius. Rebuilding of the temple has started.

Mithredath: It seems to be a couple of prophets stirring it up – Haggai and Zechariah. Always a problem when people take their religion too seriously.

Rehum: So the civic leaders – Zerubbabel and Jeshua – have got the rebuilding underway – and I have to say they're getting on at quite a pace this time.

Tattenai: But Artaxerxes' order banning it still stands? Can't we just send in the army?

Mithredath: That might be unwise – don't want to give Darius the impression we can't keep order, do we?

Rehum: So we sent the building inspectorate in – demanded names, dates, planning permission, etc. But the Jews said they were going to continue unless the new king confirms the ban. Call themselves *'servants of the God of heaven and earth'*.

Tattenai: You know, Darius might be inclined to overturn Artaxerxes' policy – he's quite religious. I don't think we should take too strong a line on this till we know his view.

Rehum: Yes, governor. I suggest that we send a letter that appears open-minded, and invite him to check the records of what Cyrus commanded.

Mithredath: Is that wise?

Rehum: My cousin is the court archivist. I suspect that particular record may not be easily found.

Tattenai: Destroying imperial records is a capital offence. Surely you are not suggesting …?

Rehum: No, no. But there are a very large number of records, and some of the slaves who file them are not too bright.

Scene 5: 6 months later

Tattenai: Ah, Shimshai. I see the imperial post arrived this morning. Have they paid my expenses claim yet?

Shimshai: Unfortunately not, governor – but there is a letter about Jerusalem.

Rehum: Confirming a ban on building I hope.

Shimshai: I'm afraid not. The palace found King Cyrus' original order.

Rehum: Found it – but where? I was assured it was not traceable in the archives.

Shimshai: Ecbatana, apparently.

Tattenai: Where?

Rehum: Let's just say it's a long camel ride from the palace.

Tattenai: So what does the letter say?

Shimshai : (reading) It forbids us to interfere with Jerusalem … And we are to provide the Jews with expenses.

Rehum: (grabbing letter) 'Whatever is needed for sacrifices must be given to the priests daily, without fail, so that they may pray for the well-being of the king and his sons.' How can you run an empire if the emperor gets religion?

Tattenai: We don't get much choice (reading): 'If anyone changes this edict, they will be killed and their house made a pile of rubble. I, Darius, have decreed it.' Let it be carried out with diligence.

Rehum: Yes, governor.

Scene 6: 4 years later

Shimshai: For your signature, governor. A letter of condolence to the widow of Councillor Mithredath.

Tattenai: Sad that he never did recover from that seizure.

Shimshai: And approval of the Invalidity pension for former Commissioner Rehum.

Tattenai: Of course.

Shimshai: A letter of congratulations to the Jewish elders on the dedication of their temple.

Tattenai: Am I going to the ceremony?

Shimshai: You would not like it, sir – rather a lot of blood sacrifices. But the court artist thought that he could picture you sending off our contribution of 100 young bulls.

Tattenai: *(looking out of window)* So I just go down to the courtyard and wave them off?

Shimshai: Yes, governor.

Kit Walkham

Nehemiah

Curriculum vitae: Nehemiah, son of Hacaliah (Nehemiah 1–14)

Address: c/o The Senior Servants' Quarters, the Royal Palace, Susa, Persia

Employment: Cupbearer and personal servant to King Artaxerxes

Duties: My main responsibility was to serve wine to the king, having first ensured that it had not been contaminated or poisoned. This work required loyalty, trustworthiness and vigilance.

I was recently seconded to oversee a major project to rebuild the walls of Jerusalem, Judah.

These duties were extensive and included:

- Project management
- Identification and assessment of needs
- Preliminary consultation with a small core group
- Compiling lists of specifications
- Drawing up plans
- Sourcing materials and potential funding
- Recruitment of suitable professionals
- On-site surveys
- Training of volunteers
- Delegation – e.g. I gave each team of workers and/or residents the responsibility for rebuilding one section of the walls.
- Motivation and team building
- Providing support on a day-to-day basis
- Organising and implementing all working procedures in order to streamline progress
- Conducting safety checks and providing regular progress reports
- Identifying problems and opposition from neighbouring regions and devising appropriate strategies to reduce the impact of these on the project.

The successful completion of this project demonstrated:

- My enthusiasm, determination and total commitment to the task
- An effective use of local knowledge – I had previously lived in Judah.
- Interpersonal skills
- The ability to team-build and boost workforce morale when necessary
- The ability to work to timelines and budgets
- Skills in dealing with conflict
- Social concern and provision for the perceived needs of the community.

I believe that my experience, strategies and personal strengths could provide a useful inspiration to others undertaking similar – although probably smaller – projects within their faith community.

Further details can be found in the Book of Nehemiah (in the Old Testament section of any Bible).

Kathy Crawford

This is our story (Nehemiah 9)

You are our God.
You are the Maker.
You made the seas and the planets.
You alone are God.

You are our God.
You keep your promises.
You walked with Abram.
You made Sarai laugh.

You are our God.
You talked with Moses.
You rescued your people out of slavery.
You made a path through the sea.

You are our God.
You led your people through the wilderness.
You fed them when they were hungry.
You gave them what they needed.

You are our God.
You gave us somewhere to live.
You gave us many children.
You gave us good things to enjoy.

You are our God.
You asked us to keep your laws and we broke them.
We chose the road to death.
We rejected the road to life.

You are our God.
This is our story.
We are slaves now.
But you have not destroyed us.

You are generous.
You are our God.
You are full of mercy.
Hear us in our distress.

Ruth Burgess

Sources and acknowledgements

'Noah's prayer (Genesis 7–8)' – by Brian Ford, from *Bare Feet and Buttercups: Resources for Ordinary Time – Trinity Sunday to the Feast of the Transfiguration*, Ruth Burgess (Ed.), 2008

'No changing history (Genesis 37)' – by Ruth Burgess, from *Bare Feet and Buttercups: Resources for Ordinary Time – Trinity Sunday to the Feast of the Transfiguration*, Ruth Burgess (Ed.), 2008

'That shine (Exodus 34:29–35)' – by Marjorie Dobson, first published on www.theworshipcloud.com, 2013

'Gossip about spies (Joshua 2:1–24)' – by Brian Ford, from *Acorns and Archangels: Resources for Ordinary Time – Feast of the Transfiguration to All Hallows'*, Ruth Burgess (Ed.), Wild Goose Publications, 2009

'Ruth and Naomi (Ruth 1)' – by Ruth Burgess, from *Acorns and Archangels: Resources for Ordinary Time – Feast of the Transfiguration to All Hallows'*, Ruth Burgess (Ed.), Wild Goose Publications, 2009

Spill the Beans material © the contributors. Spill the Beans is 'a lectionary-based resource with a Scottish flavour for Sunday Schools, Junior Churches and worship leaders': http://spillbeans.org.uk/

About the contributors

John Ablett writes as a way of understanding the patterns that underpin human lives and the symbols that shape them. He regularly contributes to *Radius Performing*, the magazine of the Religious Drama Society of Great Britain.

Angie Allport is a Deacon in the Methodist Church and, as such, is a member of the Methodist Diaconal Order. She is a pacifist and passionate about tackling all forms of injustice.

Helen Barrett: 'I have been a Methodist all my life and for the last 20 years a Local Preacher. Married with two children and three grandchildren, my other activities have included eight years as a local Councillor and 25 years as a Traidcraft Fairtrader.'

Jan Berry is a minister of the United Reformed Church who lives in Manchester. She is a writer with a particular interest in feminist spirituality and creative liturgy, and is involved in spiritual direction, workshops and retreats.

Cara Bertron works in the historic conservation field connecting people, places and ideas. After hours she writes poetry and fiction and edits *Pocket Guide*.

Ruth Burgess is a member of the Iona Community living in Dunblane. She enjoys being retired, reading detective stories, writing and editing. Her garden is graced by a murder of crows and a shy wren.

Roddy Cowie is a retired Professor of Psychology, who specialised in emotion. He is now working on self-knowledge, and a Christian understanding of emotion. He is a lay reader in the Church of Ireland and an associate of the Iona Community.

Kathy Crawford is a Reader in the Diocese of Southwell & Nottingham. She lives in Gedling with her husband and two eldest grandchildren and is, in theory, retired!

Tricia Creamer is an associate of the Iona Community and a member of Poole Methodists, where she runs a weekly 'Celtic Colours' group exploring Christian spirituality through Celtic arts. She loves writing, teaching the piano and being involved with projects which bring people together.

Liz Crumlish is a Church of Scotland minister working on Renewal. She is a Board member of RevGalBlogPals, an international supportive community for women in ministry.

Liz Delafield is a Primary school teacher. She lives in Stockport, Greater Manchester with her husband Stewart and children Jennifer and Robert.

Carol Dixon was born and brought up in Alnwick, Northumberland and is a lay preacher in the United Reformed Church. Her hymns and prayers have been published in *All Year Round*, *Songs for the New Millennium*, *Worship Live*, and the Church of Scotland Hymnbook. She is a member of the ecumenical prayer fellowship 'the Companions of Brother Lawrence', and a 'Friend of St Cuthbert's, Holy Island'. She is a wife, mother and grandmother.

Marjorie Dobson has written hymns, prayers, poems and short dramatic pieces that have been widely published and used. She is in the process of putting together a second collection of her work, to join her first, *Multi-coloured Maze* (Stainer & Bell).

Brian Ford: 'I am a retired biology teacher. As well as writing Christian poetry I also write, and act in, pantomimes, and act in amateur productions of Shakespeare.'

Mary Gibson began writing for children and adults in her local church. Her passion now is to encourage others to engage imaginatively with the Bible through verse and drama; she also enjoys gardening and choral singing. She is a former teacher.

David Hamflett is a Methodist minister and Friend of the Iona Community working in the north of England. He has a special interest in compiling and composing liturgies. He sings traditional folk songs and plays the guitar, the bodhrán and the Irish bouzouki.

Pam Hathorn: 'I am a retired teacher who enjoys reading, especially poetry and Celtic prayers, and loves the night sky and the stars.'

Deirdre Hearn: 'Born a McLean to Scottish parents in York, then living in Glasgow through the war, I attended a Quaker boarding school and learnt the value of silence. Secretarial training led to interesting jobs, voluntary work and much committee minute-taking. I was happily married to a retired tea planter but am now widowed; and in my 80s I still enjoy drawing and painting – and the company of my little dog.'

Sally Howell Johnson is a minister in the United Methodist Church in Minnesota, USA and is the author of *The Practicing Life: Simple Acts, Sacred Living* (Kirk House) and blogs at pause.hennepinchurch.org.

Ann Jepson: 'I am a retired Anglican priest living in Lancashire. I enjoy gardening and travelling and a ministry of spiritual direction and retreat giving.'

Judith Jessop: 'I am a Methodist pioneer minister living on a council estate in north Sheffield. I live a life of solitude in community and offer hospitality and an opportunity to explore spirituality to people struggling with church or with no connections to a faith-based community.'

Peter Johnston is husband of a Primary school teacher, father to four teenagers, minister of Ferryhill Parish Church in Aberdeen, editor of *Spill the Beans*, musician, blogger, and living in the mess between worry and hope.

S Anne Lawson is vicar of four parishes in rural Cheshire where she shares her vicarage with two cats, Solomon, who is as majestic as his name, and Shadow, who is tiny and lives up to his name.

Jo Love is a Resource Worker with the Wild Goose Resource Group. Her passions include long solitary walks, playing with art and words, and conversations that reach places beyond your usual after-church coffee. Her dream dinner guest would be Ecclesiastes.

Fiona Middlemist: 'I am a retired FE college librarian, an elder at Widdrington URC and a member of their worship team.'

Elisabeth Christa Miescher: 'I was active in political theology, political worship and in an ecumenical peace network in Basel, and worked for 12 years in a conference and retreat centre as Programme Director. My engagement in feminist theology led me to a Master's in Theological Studies (USA) and to a PhD in the Old Testament on Rizpah (Basel).'

Brian Morris: 'I'm an earth scientist by training, with careers in education and charity administration, a Reader at St John's Wakefield in Leeds, and a member of a hospital chaplaincy team. Now retired, I enjoy writing and landscape and wildlife photography.'

John Murning has worked in offices and industry and been a Parish Minister for 30 years, currently at Sherwood Greenlaw Church in Paisley. He is married to Linda and has two children, Sally and Jack.

Avis Palmer loves poetry and values silence. She is a volunteer for Retreat House Chester, where she leads quiet days and washes up.

Julie Rennick is a Church of Scotland minister serving in a country parish in the Scottish Borders. Her inspiration often comes when dog-walking in the hills and valleys that surround her.

Margaret Roe is a retired Methodist minister living near Lincoln. She still has an active ministry, preaching and teaching, and has recently self-published two books: *Courage, Risk and Challenge: Women of the Old Testament Tell Their Stories* (Vol. 1 and 2).

Julie Sharp went almost immediately into teaching following studying English, and remained there for 32 years. She now enjoys the chance to do voluntary work with younger children, helping them with their reading and writing. Most of her writing has been for school or church, with audiences of mixed ages, inclinations and beliefs.

Thom M Shuman is retired into transitional ministry, and continues the daily discipline of writing. He enjoys reading, silence, his family – and really misses Scotland!

Josie Smith is a member of the Ashram Community and of the United Reformed Church, where she participates in leading worship. She is presently studying for a master's degree in contextual theology.

Spill the Beans is 'a lectionary-based resource with a Scottish flavour for Sunday Schools, Junior Churches and worship leaders': http://spillbeans.org.uk

Roberta van Biezen: 'Between my first inhaled breath and my last exhaled breath I live a human life, a now 55-year-old/young woman, married, three children, soon a grandmother, in Love with Life itself, in Love with Nature.'

Liz Varley, after a long and varied life in ministry, is now a novice with the Society of the Sisters of Bethany. Our work is to pray for the unity of all Christians and to give hospitality in Jesus' name.

Kit Walkham is a Methodist local preacher in Devon, who enjoys using drama to get people thinking. She has contributed a number of sketch scripts to www.theworshipcloud.com, and is a member of the Christian network ArtServe.

Index of authors

John Ablett 73
Angie Allport 116

Helen Barrett 65
Jan Berry 47, 118, 137
Cara Bertron 46, 112, 122
Ruth Burgess 14, 16, 18, 21, 27, 37, 42, 44, 48, 57, 58, 76, 78, 81, 82, 88, 92, 97, 100, 102, 103, 124, 159, 162, 166, 170, 172, 181, 182, 188, 191, 203

Roddy Cowie 55
Kathy Crawford 135, 202
Tricia Creamer 115
Liz Crumlish 82, 107

Liz Delafield 52, 64, 165
Carol Dixon 155
Marjorie Dobson 89

Brian Ford 30, 32, 52, 56, 80, 113, 120, 136, 176

Mary Gibson 29

David Hamflett 134
Pam Hathorn 186
Deirdre Hearn 96
Sally Howell Johnson 68

Ann Jepson 89
Judith Jessop 162
Peter Johnston 35, 184

S Anne Lawson 127
Jo Love 34, 39, 74, 108, 113, 145, 147, 154, 156, 158

Fiona Middlemist 54
Elisabeth Christa Miescher 44, 150
Brian Morris 16
John Murning 69, 71, 140, 142

Avis Palmer 31

Julie Rennick 130
Margaret Roe 67

Julie Sharp 180
Thom M Shuman 93, 94, 100
Josie Smith 41
Spill the Beans (unidentified authors) 85, 86, 88, 131, 132, 149

Roberta van Biezen 36
Liz Varley 104

Kit Walkham 23, 193

Wild Goose Publications is part of the Iona Community:

- An ecumenical movement of men and women from different walks of life and different traditions in the Christian church
- Committed to the gospel of Jesus Christ, and to following where that leads, even into the unknown
- Engaged together, and with people of goodwill across the world, in acting, reflecting and praying for justice, peace and the integrity of creation
- Convinced that the inclusive community it seeks must be embodied in the community it practises

Together with its staff, the community is responsible for:

- The islands residential centres of Iona Abbey, the MacLeod Centre on Iona, and Camas Adventure Centre on the Ross of Mull

and in Glasgow:

- The administration of the Community
- Work with young people
- A publishing house, Wild Goose Publications
- Its association in the revitalising of worship with the Wild Goose Resource Group

The Iona Community was founded in Glasgow in 1938 by George MacLeod, minister, visionary and prophetic witness for peace, in the context of the poverty and despair of the Depression. Its original task of rebuilding the monastic ruins of Iona Abbey became a sign of hopeful rebuilding of community in Scotland and beyond. Today, it consists of about 280 Members, mostly in Britain, and 1500 Associate Members, with 1400 Friends worldwide. Together and apart, the community 'follows the light it has, and prays for more light'.

For information on the Iona Community contact:
The Iona Community, 21 Carlton Court, Glasgow G5 9JP, UK.
Phone: 0141 429 7281
e-mail: admin@iona.org.uk; web: www.iona.org.uk

For enquiries about visiting Iona, please contact:
Iona Abbey, Isle of Iona, Argyll PA76 6SN, UK.
Phone: 01681 700404
e-mail: enquiries@iona.org.uk

For books, CDs & digital downloads published by Wild Goose Publications: www.ionabooks.com

Wild Goose Publications, the publishing house of the Iona Community established in the Celtic Christian tradition of Saint Columba, produces books, e-books, CDs and digital downloads on:

- holistic spirituality
- social justice
- political and peace issues
- healing
- innovative approaches to worship
- song in worship, including the work of the Wild Goose Resource Group
- material for meditation and reflection

For more information:

Wild Goose Publications
21 Carlton Court,
Glasgow G5 9JP, UK

Tel. +44 (0)141 429 7281
e-mail: admin@ionabooks.com

or visit our website at
www.ionabooks.com
for details of all our products and online sales